Pasta Sauces

GENERAL EDITOR
CHUCK WILLIAMS

RECIPES
EMANUELA STUCCHI PRINETTI

PHOTOGRAPHY
ALLAN ROSENBERG

TIME
LIFE
BOOKS

Time-Life Books is a division of
TIME LIFE INCORPORATED

President and CEO: John M. Fahey, Jr.
President, Time-Life Books: John D. Hall

TIME-LIFE CUSTOM PUBLISHING

Vice President and Publisher: Terry Newell
Sales Director: Frances C. Mangan
Editorial Director: Robert A. Doyle

WILLIAMS-SONOMA
Founder/Vice-Chairman: Chuck Williams

WELDON OWEN INC.
President: John Owen
Publisher: Wendely Harvey
Managing Editor: Laurie Wertz
Copy Editor: Sharon Silva
Editorial Assistant: Janique Poncelet
Recipe Translation: Michael and Anthony Dunkley
Design: John Bull, The Book Design Company
Production: James Obata, Stephanie Sherman,
    Mick Bagnato
Food Photographer: Allan Rosenberg
Additional Food Photography: Allen V. Lott
Primary Food & Prop Stylist: Sandra Griswold
Food Stylist: Heidi Gintner
Assistant Food Stylist: Mara Barot
Glossary Illustrations: Alice Harth

The Williams-Sonoma Kitchen Library
conceived and produced by Weldon Owen Inc.
814 Montgomery St., San Francisco, CA 94133

In collaboration with Williams-Sonoma
100 North Point, San Francisco, CA 94133

Production by Mandarin Offset, Hong Kong
Printed in China

A Note on Weights and Measures:
All recipes include customary U.S. and metric
measurements. Metric conversions are based on
a standard developed for these books and have
been rounded off. Actual weights may vary.

A Weldon Owen Production

Copyright © 1994 Weldon Owen Inc.

Library of Congress
Cataloging-in-Publication Data:

Prinetti, Emanuela Stucchi.
    Pasta sauces / recipes, Emanuela Stucchi Prinetti ;
photography, Allan Rosenberg.
        p.   cm. — (Williams-Sonoma kitchen library)
    Includes index.
    ISBN 0-7835-0283-4
    1. Sauces.   2. Cookery (Pasta)   I. Title.   II. Series.
TX819.A1P75   1994
641.8'14—dc20   93-49011
                                            CIP

Contents

VEGETABLE SAUCES 15

CHEESE & EGG SAUCES 41

SEAFOOD SAUCES 61

MEAT & POULTRY SAUCES 83

INTRODUCTION

Although the term *fast food* is a modern invention, growing numbers of home cooks have discovered that it describes perfectly one of Italy's most time-honored dishes: pasta.

Go into any food store today and you'll likely find a vast selection of pastas: familiar dried strands of spaghetti and angel hair, ribbons of fettuccine and tagliatelle, shells and bow ties; unusual dried pastas like bucatini and gemelli, radiatore and ruote; and fresh or dried pastas in a rainbow of colorful flavors from spinach to tomato, chocolate to saffron. It's a simple matter to take one home, cook it in a pot of boiling water and toss it with a quickly made sauce.

Pasta is so easy to cook, in fact, that the focus of this book is not the pasta itself but the sauce that tops it. The brief introductory pages that follow cover all the fundamentals, from kitchen equipment to basic techniques for cooking and saucing pasta. Then, 45 sauce recipes are divided into chapters by their featured ingredients: vegetables, cheese and eggs, seafood, and meat and poultry.

Each recipe in this book includes suggestions for one or more pasta varieties best suited to it. But I hope you'll make these recommendations a starting point for your own explorations into the world of pasta. Check your local markets and specialty shops for new shapes and flavors from manufacturers at home and abroad. And let the suggestions for alternate ingredients lead you to invent your own pasta sauces.

I'm sure you'll be excited by how wonderfully varied and easy the world of homemade Italian-style fast food can be.

EQUIPMENT

All-purpose and special tools for putting together pasta meals in a matter of minutes

The compact array of equipment shown here epitomizes the ease and speed with which sauce-topped pasta can be prepared.

Most of the tools are all-purpose items found in any well-stocked kitchen: a food processor, knives and a cutting board for chopping or slicing ingredients; saucepans and frying pans for cooking the sauce; spoons or a whisk for stirring; and cheese graters for pasta's most popular garnish.

Some of the equipment more specifically meets the special needs of cooking pasta. A large pasta pot with a built-in strainer basket, for example, makes cooking and draining pasta easy. Italian-style pasta serving bowls hold just the right amounts attractively. Fans of freshly made pasta might also wish to treat themselves to a simple pasta machine (see page 10), which produces ready-to-cook noodles with a turn of the wrist.

1. Steamer Pan
Saucepan with insert and lid for easy steaming of vegetables.

2. Pasta Pot
Large stainless-steel pot includes strainer insert for easy draining of pasta.

3. Saucepans
Taller, narrower pan provides the best control of heat for browning garlic; larger pan is used for simmering sauces.

4. Pasta Serving Bowls
Traditional Italian-designed shallow bowls, in heavy earthenware, are the ideal shape for mixing, serving and eating pasta with sauces.

5. Wire Whisk
For stirring béchamel and other smooth or creamy sauces.

6

6. Metal Tongs
For lifting and serving pasta strands.

7. Pasta Server
Tines on long-handled metal spoon help pick up long pasta strands; slots in the server help drain excess water.

8. Slotted Spoon
For lifting cooked filled pasta, steamed shellfish and other ingredients that require draining.

9. Zester
Small, sharp holes at end of stainless-steel blade cut citrus zest into fine shreds.

10. Baking Dish
For moist or layered baked pastas intended to be served directly from the dish. Choose heavy heatproof porcelain, glazed earthenware or glass.

11. Frying Pan
For rapid sautéing, choose good-quality heavy aluminum, stainless steel, cast iron or enameled steel. Sloped, shallow sides facilitate turning and allow moisture to escape more easily for better browning.

12. Wooden Spoons
Sturdy, long-handled spoons for all-purpose stirring of sauces and other pasta toppings.

13. Mixing Bowls
Sturdy bowls in a range of sizes for combining sauce ingredients. Can be made of earthenware, porcelain, glass or stainless steel.

14. Food Processor
Stainless-steel metal blade chops large quantities of ingredients or purées sauces.

15. Colander
For draining pasta or for straining solids from stock.

16. Chef's Knife and Paring Knife
Larger all-purpose chef's knife for general chopping and slicing of sauce ingredients. Smaller paring knife for peeling vegetables and cutting up small ingredients. Choose sturdy knives with sharp stainless-steel blades securely attached to sturdy handles that feel comfortable in the hand.

17. Pot Holder and Oven Glove
Heavy-duty cotton provides good protection from hot cookware.

18. Cheese Graters
Rotary or half-cylindrical models quickly shred or grate hard cheeses such as Parmesan.

19. Cutting Board
Choose one made of tough but resilient white acrylic, which is nonporous and cleans easily. Thoroughly clean the chopping surface after every use.

Pasta Basics

Simple guidelines to ensure perfectly cooked, precisely portioned pasta meals

A quick glance through the pasta sauce recipes in this book will show that the pasta itself is absent from the ingredient lists. The reason is simple and purposeful: These sauces are meant to be versatile, something you can prepare quickly and spoon over or mix with any pasta of your choosing. And while the introductory note to each recipe suggests pasta varieties particularly well suited to the sauce, the final decision is entirely your own. (You'll find a guide to pasta shapes in the glossary on page 106.)

But there's another good reason for not including the pasta instructions in each sauce recipe: Cooking pasta is so easy that telling you how to do it time and again would be needlessly repetitious. The following guidelines, along with the photographs on the opposite page, are all you need to know to prepare pasta at its best.

How Much to Prepare?

Each of the pasta sauce recipes in this book yields four ample main-course portions. If you wish to offer the dish as a first course, the quantities will serve up to six.

Because it is hard for many people to estimate visually the number of servings packaged dried or fresh pasta will yield, pasta manufacturers are diligent about providing that information on the package. But, as a general guideline, you'll need about 1 pound (500 g) dried pasta for 4 main-course or 6 first-course servings. Because fresh pasta is moister and therefore absorbs less water during cooking, you'll need no more than about ¾ pound (375 g) for the same number of servings.

Cooking the Pasta "al Dente"

To let the pasta circulate freely as it cooks, begin with a sufficient quantity of water. For the quantities mentioned above, 5 quarts (5 l) of water are adequate. Add about 1½ tablespoons salt to the water before heating it; if you're on a salt-restricted diet, eliminate it from the sauce itself rather than from the pasta cooking water. Bring the water to a full rolling boil before adding the pasta.

Cooking time will vary with the pasta's shape, size and dryness; check suggested times on the packaging. Fresh pasta usually takes 1–3 minutes; dried is generally ready in 7–15 minutes.

To test pasta for doneness, remove a piece from the pot at the earliest moment it might be ready; let it cool briefly, then bite into it. Perfectly cooked pasta is done al dente—an Italian term meaning "to the tooth," or tender but firm. If you look at the piece you bite into, its very center should look a tiny bit opaque. If your first sample seems too chewy, wait another minute and test again.

Some recipes in this book in which the pasta completes cooking in its sauce (see sidebar, opposite page) call for it to be done "almost al dente." In such cases, the pasta should be drained a minute or two before it is done, at which point it will be very chewy.

If the pasta will be used in a cold dish, never cool it by rinsing under cold water; doing so will turn the pasta gummy or mushy. Instead, drain the pasta well, toss lightly with a little extra-virgin olive oil and let it cool to room temperature.

1. Boiling the water.
Bring a generous quantity of salted water to a boil in a large pot. When a full, rolling boil is reached, add the pasta; if the boil subsides, cover the pot briefly to help raise the heat. Stir the pasta occasionally to prevent the strands from sticking together.

2. Testing for doneness.
Cook until the pasta is al dente—tender but still firm. To test, remove a piece with tongs, a pasta server or a slotted spoon at the earliest moment the pasta might be ready; let it cool slightly, then taste.

3. Draining the pasta.
If using a pasta pot with a strainer insert, as shown here, simply grasp the strainer basket's handles and lift it out. Alternatively, pour the contents of the pot into a colander set inside the kitchen sink. Shake the strainer or colander to remove any remaining water.

BLENDING THE FLAVORS OF PASTA AND SAUCE

A traditional Italian pasta-cooking method known as *mantecare* is used in some recipes in this book to allow pasta to absorb more of the flavors of its sauce. The pasta is only partially boiled and is then added to the sauce—along with a bit of the boiling water if needed to facilitate mixing—to complete its cooking in the sauce itself.

1. Adding pasta to the pan.
Cook the pasta until almost al dente—a minute or two short of its usual cooking time. Drain well, reserving a little of its cooking liquid. Add the pasta to the prepared sauce.

2. Blending pasta and sauce.
Using a pair of wooden spoons or pasta servers, gently toss together the pasta and sauce; add a splash or two of cooking liquid if necessary to facilitate blending. Simmer a few minutes more until the pasta is done al dente.

Red and Green Sauce

FRESH PASTA

Easy to prepare at home, fresh pasta made from an egg-and-flour dough can be ready to cook and eat in a matter of minutes. Whether you make it by hand or use a pasta machine, mixing, kneading, rolling out and cutting a variety of pasta strands—from thin angel hair to wider tagliatelle or fettuccine ribbons—can be an enjoyable and rewarding task. But don't fall into the trap of thinking that it is necessarily better than dried pasta. Any Italian will tell you that fresh and dried are different, equally good eating experiences.

The proportions given below for fresh pasta ingredients are approximate, and may vary with the actual size of the eggs you use, how you measure the flour, the absorbency of the flour, and how dry or humid the weather is when you make the pasta. In the end, your eyes and your hands are the best judges of how the dough is proceeding.

If you don't have the time to make your own fresh pasta, visit your local Italian delicatessen or the refrigerated display in the food store. Fresh pasta in a wide variety of shapes and flavors is becoming increasingly available as a commercial product, ready to take home and cook in an instant.

Keep store-bought fresh pasta in the refrigerator and use it within the time indicated on the package. Your own freshly made and cut pasta may be left at room temperature until completely dry, and will then keep for up to a week at cool room temperature in a covered container; the dry pasta may also be wrapped airtight and refrigerated for up to 1 week or frozen for up to 3 months.

INGREDIENTS FOR PASTA DOUGH:

2 cups (10 oz/300 g) all-purpose (plain) flour, plus
⅓ cup (2 oz/60 g) for board and sprinkling
3 eggs

Makes about 1 lb (500 g)

FRESH PASTA BY HAND

1. Mixing and kneading the dough.
On a work surface using a fork, or in a food processor, combine the flour and eggs to form a dough. With the palm and heel of your hand, knead the dough until smooth and elastic, at least 5 minutes. If dough sticks or seems a little soft, sprinkle with flour.

2. Rolling out the dough.
On a clean work surface dusted with flour, flatten the dough with your hand. Using a flour-dusted rolling pin, roll out the dough thinly.

3. Cutting the pasta by hand.
Loosely roll up pasta around rolling pin and unroll onto a flour-dusted kitchen towel, leaving it until dry to the touch but still flexible, about 10 minutes, or less if the air is very dry. On the work surface, roll pasta up into a cylinder and cut crosswise into ribbons of desired width.

FRESH PASTA BY MACHINE

Mix and knead the dough, then cut into 6 portions. Lightly dust a portion and crank through the rollers of a pasta machine adjusted to the widest setting. Dust, fold into thirds, adjust the rollers a notch narrower, and roll again; repeat until desired thinness is reached. Secure the cutting attachment and guide the sheet of pasta through to cut pasta strands (shown here).

BASIC & SIMPLE SAUCES

Some sauces, such as those on this and the following two pages, are so simple that they are hardly recipes at all—being nothing more than rapid sautés or simmers of a few fresh, flavorful ingredients that naturally highlight the mild, earthy taste of pasta. Use them as the starting points for your own imaginative pasta sauce creations.

GARLIC, OIL AND CAYENNE PEPPER SAUCE

Many Italian recipes start with sautéing garlic in olive oil; this sauce begins and ends with that step, producing a simple, aromatic topping for spaghetti or the finer fedelini, to create a favorite late-night snack in Italy called spaghetti aglio e olio. Careful timing is essential to ensure that the sauce is done at the same moment the al dente pasta is cooked and drained; there should be an audible sizzle when they are combined. To achieve this result, peel and slice the garlic while the pasta's cooking water is heating; and begin heating the olive oil the moment the pasta is put in the boiling water.

¼ cup (2 fl oz/60 ml) extra-virgin olive oil
4 cloves garlic, very finely sliced
pinch of cayenne pepper
salt

Add your choice of pasta to boiling water.

In a tall, narrow saucepan over medium heat, warm the olive oil. Add the garlic and cayenne pepper, reduce the heat to very low and cook very slowly, stirring, so the garlic takes on its distinctive golden color without burning, about 5 minutes.

Drain the pasta and transfer to a warmed serving dish. Raise the heat under the garlic sauce for a few seconds to heat it as much as possible without further coloring the garlic. Immediately pour it over the pasta. Season to taste with salt and serve at once.

Serves 4

SAUTÉING GARLIC

An essential element of so many pasta sauces, garlic develops a richer, mellower, more aromatic flavor when it is slowly sautéed until golden brown. But special care must be taken to ensure that it does not overcook, blacken and turn bitter.

1. Heating oil and garlic.
Put extra-virgin olive oil in a saucepan that is tall and narrow—the better to control the heat. Set the heat to medium and, when the oil is hot, add the garlic.

2. Sautéing until done.
Reduce the heat to low and sauté, stirring with a spoon, until the garlic turns a light but uniform gold. Remove from the heat immediately.

SIMPLE TOMATO SAUCE

A few basic ingredients are all it takes to highlight the sweet taste of peak-of-season tomatoes in this easy sauce. It's marvelous with all fresh egg pastas, especially fettuccine and tagliatelle; with multicolored linguine; and, traditionally, with potato gnocchi. Make sure the tomatoes are the ripest and best quality you can find, and use only fresh basil, which is more aromatic than the dried herb. If the tomatoes' flavor is a bit acidic, add a tiny spoonful of sugar to perk them up. The butter in this recipe is typical of northern Italian cooking; substitute olive oil, if you wish.

⅓ cup (3 oz/90 g) unsalted butter
1 small white onion, thinly sliced crosswise
3–4 tablespoons water
1 lb (500 g) fresh plum (Roma) tomatoes, peeled, sliced lengthwise and seeded, or canned plum tomatoes, drained and chopped
salt
8 fresh basil leaves, torn into small pieces
¾ cup (3 oz/90 g) freshly grated Parmesan cheese

In a large frying pan over medium heat, melt the butter. Add the onion and the water, cover and cook gently, stirring occasionally, until tender and completely translucent, about 10 minutes. (Adding the water and covering the pan helps to keep the onion from burning.)

Add the tomatoes, cover partially and cook over low heat until a creamy consistency is achieved, about 20 minutes. (How long this step takes will depend upon how much water the tomatoes contain.) If the sauce begins to dry out too much before the creamy state is achieved, add a few tablespoons water to the pan.

Add salt to taste and the basil and stir well. Remove from the heat and let stand, covered, for a few minutes so the basil can release its aroma.

Meanwhile, cook your choice of pasta until al dente. Drain and transfer to a warmed serving dish. Immediately pour the sauce over the pasta and toss well. Serve at once. Pass the Parmesan cheese at the table.

Serves 4

Tomatoes with Aromatic Vegetables

Simple Tomato Sauce

Tomatoes with Aromatic Vegetables

Although this sauce from central and southern Italy is delicious on all kinds of dried pasta, it's at its best with spaghetti. Use just a little oil and medium-high heat for sautéing the vegetables, taking care that they brown nicely without burning.

1 clove garlic
1 small carrot, peeled and coarsely chopped
½ small red (Spanish) onion, coarsely chopped
1 celery stalk, coarsely chopped
1 bay leaf
¼ cup (2 fl oz/60 ml) extra-virgin olive oil
1 lb (500 g) fresh plum (Roma) tomatoes, peeled, sliced
   lengthwise and seeded, or canned plum tomatoes,
   drained and chopped
1 tablespoon dried oregano
salt
freshly ground pepper
¾ cup (3 oz/90 g) freshly grated Parmesan cheese

*I*n a food processor fitted with the metal blade, combine the garlic, carrot, onion, celery and bay leaf. Pulse to chop more finely.

In a wide frying pan over medium heat, warm the olive oil. Add the chopped vegetables and raise the heat to medium-high. Stirring frequently with a wooden spoon, cook until the vegetables begin to turn golden, 10 minutes or longer.

Add the tomatoes, oregano and salt and pepper to taste; reduce the heat to low, cover partially and cook until a creamy consistency forms, 30 minutes longer. If the sauce begins to dry out too much before the creamy state is achieved, add a few tablespoons water to the pan.

Meanwhile, cook your choice of pasta until al dente. Drain and transfer to a warmed serving dish. Immediately pour the sauce over the pasta, toss well and serve at once. Pass the Parmesan cheese at the table.

Serves 4

A Sampler of Simple Sauces

Using extra-virgin olive oil or unsalted butter as your starting point, you can easily come up with a wide range of sauces and toppings for pasta. Here are some ideas to get you started.

◎ Heat oil and add chopped fresh tomatoes, sliced green or black olives and chopped fresh basil.

◎ Heat oil and sauté finely chopped garlic and thinly sliced or shredded zucchini (courgettes); toss with pasta and freshly grated Parmesan cheese.

◎ Heat oil and sauté chopped garlic and whole fresh sage leaves; toss with pasta, freshly ground pepper and freshly grated pecorino cheese.

◎ Heat oil and sauté chopped garlic and red pepper flakes with broccoli florets.

◎ Heat oil and sauté finely chopped garlic and red pepper flakes; toss with pasta and finely chopped mixed fresh herbs such as basil, parsley, tarragon and oregano.

◎ Toss pasta with melted butter and lots of freshly grated Parmesan cheese.

◎ Toss pasta with melted butter, parboiled peas, chopped fresh tarragon and freshly grated Parmesan cheese.

◎ Simmer heavy (double) cream and add chopped cooked ham; toss with pasta and lots of freshly grated Parmesan cheese.

◎ Heat oil and sauté finely chopped garlic, anchovies and chopped fresh oregano.

Eggplant with Toasted Bread Crumbs

MELANZANE E PANGRATTATO

¾ cup (6 fl oz/180 ml) extra-virgin
   olive oil

2 cloves garlic, thinly sliced

¾ lb (375 g) fresh plum (Roma)
   tomatoes, peeled and chopped, or
   canned plum tomatoes, drained
   and chopped

2 tablespoons chopped fresh basil

pinch of cayenne pepper

salt

2 Asian (slender) eggplants
   (aubergines), about ¾ lb (375 g)
   total weight, trimmed and cut
   crosswise into slices about ¼ inch
   (6 mm) thick

6 oz (180 g) fairly stale coarse country
   bread, crusts discarded and bread
   crumbled

In a popular Sicilian version of this recipe, the eggplant is fried until golden in an abundance of extra-virgin olive oil and then patted dry with paper towels. The finished pasta is then topped with freshly grated pecorino or provolone cheese in place of the bread crumbs. For either approach, spaghetti is traditional. Feel free to use globe eggplants if you prefer.

*I*n a frying pan over medium heat, warm ¼ cup (2 fl oz/ 60 ml) of the olive oil. Add the garlic, raise the heat to high and sauté until golden, a couple of minutes. Add the tomatoes, basil, cayenne pepper and salt to taste. Cook uncovered over medium heat, stirring occasionally, about 15 minutes.

At the same time, in a separate frying pan over medium heat, warm ¼ cup (2 fl oz/60 ml) of the olive oil. Add the eggplant and sauté, stirring often, until tender, about 15 minutes.

In yet another frying pan over medium heat, warm the remaining ¼ cup (2 fl oz/60 ml) olive oil. Add the bread crumbs and toast, stirring often, until they turn golden, a couple of minutes.

Meanwhile, cook your choice of pasta until al dente. Drain and transfer to a warmed serving dish. Immediately pour the eggplant and tomato mixtures over the pasta and toss well. Sprinkle with the hot bread crumbs and serve at once.

Serves 4

Artichokes with Mint and Parsley

CARCIOFI CON MENTA E PREZZEMOLO

juice of 1 lemon

8 artichokes, about 3 oz (90 g) each

¼ cup (2 fl oz/60 ml) extra-virgin olive oil

2 cloves garlic, thinly sliced

¼ cup (2 fl oz/60 ml) water

1 tablespoon chopped fresh mint

1 tablespoon chopped fresh flat-leaf (Italian) parsley

salt

freshly ground white pepper

½ cup (2 oz/60 g) freshly grated Parmesan cheese

Because the pasta in this recipe is cooked twice—once in boiling water and then briefly in oil—you need a fairly robust shape that will hold up well. Penne and radiatori are good choices. Asparagus tips, parboiled until tender-crisp before they go into the frying pan, can be used instead of artichokes.

*H*ave ready a large bowl three-fourths full of water to which you have added the lemon juice. Remove the stem and the tough outer leaves from the artichokes until you reach the pale green heart. Cut each artichoke in half lengthwise. Scoop out the prickly choke from the center and discard. Cut the artichokes lengthwise into long, thin slices. As the artichokes are cut, place them in the bowl of water.

In a large frying pan over medium heat, warm the olive oil. Add the garlic and sauté, stirring, until browned, about 3 minutes. Drain the artichokes, pat them dry and add to the pan. Raise the heat to high and sauté, stirring, for a few minutes. Add the ¼ cup (2 fl oz/60 ml) water and continue cooking over high heat until the water is absorbed, 6–7 minutes.

Meanwhile, cook your choice of pasta until almost al dente. Drain the pasta, reserving about ¼ cup (2 fl oz/60 ml) of the cooking water. Add the pasta and the reserved hot cooking water to the artichokes in the frying pan along with the mint, parsley and salt and white pepper to taste. Finish cooking over high heat, stirring constantly, for 1–2 minutes.

Transfer to a warmed serving dish, top with the Parmesan cheese and toss well. Serve immediately.

Serves 4

Cherry Tomatoes with Basil
POMODORO FRESCO ALLA ROMANA

1 lb (500 g) cherry tomatoes
coarse salt
6 tablespoons (3 fl oz/90 ml) extra-
  virgin olive oil
5 cloves garlic, thinly sliced
pinch of cayenne pepper
12 fresh basil leaves, torn into small
  pieces

The success of this quick recipe—a classic topping for spaghetti—depends upon finding sun-ripened, sweet and flavorful cherry tomatoes. For a more substantial dish, add ¼ pound (120 g) mozzarella cheese, cut into 1-inch (2.5-cm) cubes and tossed into the pasta with the tomatoes.

Place a saucepan half full of water over high heat and bring to a boil. Drop the tomatoes into the boiling water and heat for 1 minute. Drain and peel while still hot. Cut the tomatoes in half and place in a sieve. Sprinkle with coarse salt and let stand for 30 minutes to drain off the excess liquid.

Add your choice of pasta to boiling water. At the same time, in a tall, narrow saucepan over medium heat, warm the olive oil. Add the garlic and cayenne pepper, reduce the heat to very low and cook very slowly, stirring, so the garlic takes on its distinctive golden color without burning, about 5 minutes.

When the pasta is al dente, drain and transfer to a warmed serving dish. Immediately add the tomatoes and basil to the dish. Raise the heat under the garlic sauce for a few seconds to heat it as much as possible without further coloring the garlic, then pour it over the pasta and toss well. Serve at once.

Serves 4

Chick-peas and Cabbage
Ceci e Cavolo

⅔ cup (5 oz/150 g) dried chick-peas
    (garbanzo beans)
1 celery stalk, sliced
¼ cup (2 fl oz/60 ml) extra-virgin
    olive oil
1 red (Spanish) onion, sliced
1 head Savoy cabbage, about ¾ lb
    (375 g), cored and chopped
5 or 6 dried shiitake mushrooms,
    soaked in warm water to cover until
    softened, about 30 minutes
salt
freshly ground pepper
¾ cup (3 oz/90 g) freshly grated
    pecorino cheese

The robust combination of beans and vegetables turns a simple bowl of rigatoni or other large pasta shapes into a complete, healthful meal. You can substitute dried lentils or cranberry (borlotto) or fava (broad) beans for the chick-peas, or use a mixture. Dried beans take a long time to cook; lentils, which do not require soaking, cook relatively quickly. If you like, use a pressure cooker to cut the time by about a third.

❧

Place the chick-peas in a bowl, add water to cover and soak for 12 hours at room temperature, changing the water a few times.

Drain the chick-peas and place in a saucepan. Add the celery, olive oil, onion, cabbage and water to cover by several inches. Bring to a boil, reduce the heat to low, cover partially and simmer until the chick-peas are very tender, about 3 hours. If the chick-peas begin to dry out before they are tender, add a little lukewarm water to the pan.

When the chick-peas are almost ready, drain the mushrooms and remove their stems and discard. Slice the mushrooms and add to the chick-peas. Then, using a fork, mash a few of the chick-peas to thicken the sauce. Season to taste with salt and pepper.

Meanwhile, cook your choice of pasta until al dente. Drain and transfer to a warmed serving dish. Immediately add the sauce and grated pecorino; toss well. Serve at once.

Serves 4

Pumpkin with Sage

ZUCCA E SALVIA

1 piece pumpkin, about 1 lb (500 g)
⅓ cup (3 oz/90 g) unsalted butter
1 white onion, sliced paper-thin
8 fresh sage leaves
¾ cup (3 oz/90 g) freshly grated
   Parmesan cheese
salt
freshly ground white pepper

With its vibrant color and mild, slightly sweet flavor, pumpkin goes beautifully with such egg ribbons as tagliatelle or fettuccine, and is especially lovely with green spinach pastas. For a more exotic flavor, add a hint of grated nutmeg and a crumbled amaretto cookie.

Peel the piece of pumpkin; remove any seeds and strings and discard. Cut the pumpkin into finger-width slices, then cut the slices into small cubes; you should have about 3 cups. Set aside.

In a large, wide frying pan over medium heat, melt half of the butter. Add the onion and sauté, stirring, until it is translucent, about 10 minutes. Add the pumpkin, raise the heat a little and cook, stirring often, until tender, about 20 minutes longer.

When the pumpkin is almost ready, melt the remaining butter in another frying pan over medium-high heat. Add the sage leaves and fry until they are slightly crisp, just a few minutes.

Meanwhile, cook your choice of pasta until al dente. Drain and transfer to a warmed serving dish. Immediately pour the pumpkin sauce over the pasta. Add the Parmesan and salt and white pepper to taste and toss well. Pour on the sage and butter and serve at once.

Serves 4

Tomatoes and White Wine
SALSA DI POMODORO AL VINO BIANCO

6 tablespoons (3 fl oz/90 ml) extra-
virgin olive oil
3 or 4 cloves garlic, finely chopped
½ cup (4 fl oz/125 ml) dry white wine
1½ lb (750 g) fresh plum (Roma)
tomatoes, peeled and chopped, or
canned plum tomatoes, drained and
chopped
salt
freshly ground white pepper

So pure are the flavors of this sauce for spaghetti or fedelini that they're at their tastiest without the addition of cheese. Because of the simplicity of this sauce, it is best to prepare it with juicy, flavorful fresh tomatoes. When adding the wine to the hot oil, do so carefully, as it will splatter.

*I*n a frying pan over medium heat, warm the olive oil. Add the garlic, reduce the heat to very low and cook very slowly so the garlic takes on its distinctive golden color without burning, about 5 minutes.

Add the white wine, raise the heat to high and cook until the wine evaporates, 2–3 minutes. Add the tomatoes, salt to taste and plenty of white pepper. Cook uncovered, stirring often, until light and slightly thickened, about 5 minutes.

Meanwhile, cook your choice of pasta until al dente. Drain and transfer to a warmed serving dish. Immediately pour the sauce over the pasta and serve at once.

Serves 4

Potatoes and Arugula
PATATE E RUCOLA

salt

10 oz (300 g) baking potatoes, peeled
and cut into ⅓-inch (1-cm) cubes

¾ lb (375 g) arugula (rocket), cut into
long, thin strips

6 tablespoons (3 fl oz/90 ml) extra-
virgin olive oil

1 clove garlic

pinch of cayenne pepper

*Use plain or spinach radiatori or armoniche pasta. For a
richer version, add 2 or 3 ripe plum (Roma) tomatoes, peeled;
2 anchovy fillets; and 2 tablespoons drained capers, all finely
chopped together, to the garlic and oil.*

*F*ill a large saucepan three-fourths full of water. Bring to a
boil and add salt to taste, the potato cubes and arugula.
When the water returns to the boil, add your choice of
pasta and cook until almost al dente.

Meanwhile, in a tall, narrow saucepan over medium heat,
warm the olive oil. Add the garlic and cayenne pepper,
reduce the heat to very low and cook very slowly so the
garlic takes on its distinctive golden color without burning,
about 5 minutes.

Drain the pasta and vegetables and transfer to a warmed
serving dish. Raise the heat under the garlic sauce for a few
seconds to heat it as much as possible without further
coloring the garlic. Discard the garlic. Immediately pour
the oil over the pasta and toss well. Serve at once.

Serves 4

Sun-Dried Tomatoes with Green Olives

SALSA ROSA

¾ cup (6 fl oz/180 ml) heavy (double)
  cream
12 green olives, pitted and finely
  chopped
4 oz (125 g) sun-dried tomatoes in olive
  oil, drained and finely chopped
salt
freshly ground pepper
¾ cup (3 oz/90 g) freshly grated
  Parmesan cheese

So intense are the flavors of sun-dried tomatoes and green olives that this sauce requires little if any additional seasoning. This recipe is particularly good with such pasta shapes as farfalle and shells, because they trap the sauce in their hollows. For an interesting variation, use extra-virgin olive oil in place of the cream, and instead of heating the ingredients, simply purée them in a food processor or blender to make a pestolike topping. A few capers can be added to the sauce, if you like.

Add your choice of pasta to boiling water. When it is almost cooked, combine the cream, olives and sun-dried tomatoes in a frying pan over very low heat. Heat just until the cream is lukewarm and slightly pink.

Drain the pasta as soon as it is al dente, reserving about ¼ cup (2 fl oz/60 ml) of the cooking water. Stir the reserved hot cooking water into the cream sauce.

Transfer the pasta to a warmed serving dish. Immediately pour the cream sauce over the pasta; add salt and pepper to taste and the Parmesan cheese. Toss well. Serve at once.

Serves 4

Red and Green Sauce
VERDE E ROSSO

4 tablespoons (2 fl oz/60 ml) extra-
  virgin olive oil
1 white onion, sliced
1 clove garlic, sliced
2 carrots, peeled and cut into thin strips
1 red bell pepper (capsicum), seeded,
  deribbed and cut into thin strips
10 oz (300 g) fresh plum (Roma)
  tomatoes, peeled and chopped, or
  canned plum tomatoes, drained and
  chopped
1 tablespoon dried oregano
salt
2 tablespoons chopped flat-leaf (Italian)
  parsley
1 tablespoon chopped fresh basil
¾ cup (3 oz/90 g) freshly grated
  Parmesan cheese, optional

*Red tomatoes and green herbs combine to make a vibrantly
perfumed sauce that is ideal on fresh or dried tagliatelle or
fettuccine. For an additional touch of color, use green spinach
pasta. Replace the carrots with zucchini (courgettes), if you wish.*

*I*n a large frying pan over high heat, warm 2 tablespoons
of the olive oil. Add the onion and garlic and sauté until
beginning to soften, 3–4 minutes. Add the carrot and bell
pepper strips and continue cooking over high heat a few
minutes longer. Add the tomatoes, oregano and salt to taste
and reduce the heat to low. Cook uncovered, stirring
occasionally, until the liquid evaporates and the vegetables
are tender, 10 minutes longer.

Meanwhile, cook your choice of pasta until almost al
dente. Drain and add to the sauce in the frying pan.
Finish cooking over high heat, stirring constantly, for
1–2 minutes. Turn off the heat and mix in the remaining
2 tablespoons olive oil.

Transfer the pasta to a warmed serving dish. Sprinkle
with the parsley and basil and serve at once. Pass the
Parmesan cheese at the table, if desired.

Serves 4

Green Beans and Saffron
FAGIOLINI E ZAFFERANO

7 oz (200 g) romano beans

¼ cup (2 fl oz/60 ml) extra-virgin
olive oil

2 medium-sized white onions, thinly
sliced

2 pinches of saffron threads, soaked in
1 tablespoon hot water

2 egg yolks, lightly beaten

salt

freshly ground pepper

¾ cup (3 oz/90 g) freshly grated
pecorino cheese

2 tablespoons chopped fresh flat-leaf
(Italian) parsley

This colorful green-and-yellow topping pairs well with garganelli (shown here) or regular or spinach penne. Romano beans, sometimes called Italian beans, are flat, flavorful green beans. If unavailable, substitute regular green beans or runner beans. Alternative vegetables include an equal weight of shelled peas or, for an unusual touch, 8 zucchini (courgette) blossoms.

Trim off the ends of the beans, then slice on the diagonal into diamond-shaped pieces about ⅓ inch (1 cm) long. Set aside.

In a large, wide frying pan over medium heat, warm the olive oil. Add the onion and the saffron and its soaking water and sauté for a few minutes until the onion begins to soften. Add the beans and sauté over high heat, stirring continuously, for a couple of minutes.

Meanwhile, cook your choice of pasta until almost al dente. Drain, reserving about ½ cup (4 fl oz/125 ml) of the cooking water. Add the pasta to the sauce in the frying pan, along with the egg yolks, salt and pepper to taste and the reserved hot cooking water. Raise the heat to high and finish cooking, stirring vigorously, for 1–2 minutes.

Remove from the heat, add the pecorino cheese and toss well. Transfer to a warmed serving dish, sprinkle with the parsley and serve immediately.

Serves 4

Onion Cream Sauce with Black Olives

CREMA DI CIPOLLE E OLIVE

1¼ lb (600 g) white onions, sliced
¼ cup (2 oz/60 g) unsalted butter
salt
freshly ground pepper
¾ cup (6 fl oz/180 ml) heavy (double)
  cream
¾ cup (3 oz/90 g) freshly grated
  Parmesan cheese
15 black olives such as Gaeta, pitted
  and sliced

The pungent flavors of black olives and onion complement each other in this creamy sauce for fresh egg pasta or dried pasta strands such as linguine. To enhance the onion flavor, add a small pinch of sugar as you sauté them. For the olives, you can substitute ¾ cup (4 oz/125 g) shelled peas, boiled for a few minutes and drained, along with small cubes of cooked ham.

*F*ill a saucepan three-fourths full of water and bring to a boil. Add the onions and boil for 5 minutes. Drain well.

In a large frying pan over low heat, melt the butter. Add the drained onions and salt and pepper to taste and sauté, stirring often, until translucent and tender, about 20 minutes. Add a little water from time to time if the onions begin to stick. Add the cream and cook, stirring, a few minutes longer over low heat.

Meanwhile, add your choice of pasta to boiling water. Transfer the hot onion mixture to a blender or a food processor fitted with the metal blade and blend until creamy.

When the pasta is al dente, drain and transfer to a warmed serving dish. Immediately add the hot puréed sauce, Parmesan cheese and olives and toss well. Serve at once.

Serves 4

Red Bell Pepper Purée
CREMA DI PEPERONI

3 red bell peppers (capsicums)
1 clove garlic
¼ cup (2 fl oz/60 ml) extra-virgin
  olive oil
salt
2 tablespoons chopped flat-leaf (Italian)
  parsley

The naturally sweet flavor of roasted red bell peppers comes through in this easy preparation, ideal on spaghetti. The dish is also wonderful served chilled: purée 1 celery stalk (chopped first) with the sauce ingredients, toss with the pasta and chill.

Preheat an oven to 350°F (180°C).

Arrange the bell peppers on a baking sheet. Place in the oven and cook, turning occasionally, until completely soft and blistered evenly, about 30 minutes. Remove the peppers from the oven and, when cool enough to handle, peel them. Stem the peppers and remove the seeds and ribs.

Place the peppers in a food processor fitted with the metal blade or in a blender. Add the garlic, olive oil and salt to taste. Process until smooth.

Meanwhile, cook your choice of pasta until al dente. Drain and transfer to a warmed serving dish. Immediately pour the purée over the top and toss well. Sprinkle with the parsley and serve at once.

Serves 4

Walnuts and Rosemary

Noci e Rosmarino

¼ cup (2 fl oz/60 ml) extra-virgin
  olive oil
2 cloves garlic, sliced paper-thin
4 anchovy fillets packed in olive oil,
  drained and lightly mashed
pinch of cayenne pepper
½ cup (2 oz/60 g) walnut pieces
1 tablespoon chopped fresh rosemary
salt
freshly ground green peppercorns
½ cup (2 oz/60 g) freshly grated
  Parmesan cheese

*This sauce is ideal with fusilli or other spirals, or with angel
hair pasta. It makes a lovely first course to precede fish. For a
spicier sauce, omit the Parmesan, add a little more cayenne and
top with freshly chopped Italian parsley.*

Add your choice of pasta to boiling water.

In a tall, narrow saucepan over medium heat, warm the
olive oil. Add the garlic, anchovies and cayenne pepper,
reduce the heat to very low and cook very slowly, stirring,
so the garlic takes on its distinctive golden color without
burning, about 5 minutes.

Add half of the walnuts and all of the rosemary. Leave
the mixture to heat for a few seconds.

When the pasta is al dente, drain and transfer to a
warmed serving dish. Immediately pour the sauce over the
pasta and add the remaining nuts. Season to taste with salt
and green pepper and toss well. Sprinkle with the
Parmesan cheese and serve at once.

Serves 4

Ricotta with Ham and Corn
RICOTTA CON PROSCIUTTO E GRANTURCO

salt

2 ears white or yellow corn, shucked

¾ cup (6½ oz/200 g) ricotta cheese

¼ cup (2 oz/60 g) unsalted butter, at room temperature

3 oz (90 g) cooked ham, cut into thin strips

freshly ground white pepper

¾ cup (3 oz/90 g) freshly grated Parmesan cheese

During summer's heat, try serving this satisfying dish luke-warm. Farfalle are the ideal pasta for this creamy sauce; other shapes of similar size will work well, too. A few coarsely chopped hazelnuts (filberts) add extra texture and taste, and 1 teaspoon chopped fresh chives contributes a colorful garnish.

ʃʃʃ

Bring a large saucepan three-fourths full of water to a rolling boil. Add salt to taste and the corn and remove from the heat. Cover and let stand for 5 minutes. Remove the corn from the water. Using a sharp knife, slice off the kernels. Set aside.

Cook your choice of pasta until al dente. While the pasta is cooking, place the ricotta in a bowl, add a few table-spoons of hot pasta cooking water and stir until the cheese is smooth and creamy.

Drain the pasta and transfer to a warmed serving dish. Immediately add the butter, ham, ricotta and salt and white pepper to taste. Toss well, sprinkle with the corn and serve. Pass the Parmesan cheese at the table.

Serves 4

Goat Cheese and Celery with Black Olives

CAPRINO E SEDANO

8 tablespoons (4 fl oz/125 ml) extra-
virgin olive oil
3 celery stalks, trimmed and thinly
sliced
6 oz (185 g) fresh goat cheese,
crumbled
salt
freshly ground pepper
16 black olives such as Kalamata, pitted
small bunch of tiny fresh basil leaves

Tossed together in just a few minutes, this cold pasta dish may be made with eye-catching shapes such as fusilli or small shells, or simply with penne. If you like, substitute provolone or pecorino (cut into small cubes) for the goat cheese. Add a handful of tiny cherry tomatoes to enliven the recipe further.

~~~~

Cook your choice of pasta until al dente. Drain and place in a bowl. Add 2 tablespoons of the olive oil and toss well. Let cool to room temperature, stirring every so often.

Transfer the cooled pasta to a serving dish and add the remaining 6 tablespoons (3 fl oz/90 ml) oil, the celery, goat cheese and salt and pepper to taste. Toss well. Sprinkle with the olives and garnish with basil leaves. Serve at once. Or, if you like, chill in the refrigerator for 1 hour before serving.

Serves 4

Cauliflower and Gruyère
CAVOLFIORE E GROVIERA

2 cups (16 fl oz/500 ml) milk
3½ tablespoons unsalted butter
3½ tablespoons all-purpose (plain) flour
salt
freshly grated nutmeg
1 small head cauliflower, about 1 lb
   (500 g), trimmed and divided into
   florets
½ cup (2 oz/60 g) shredded Gruyère
   cheese

This favorite vegetable-and-cheese combination is excellent with a pasta shape such as rigatoni, which holds its form well during baking. Other types of Swiss cheese can be substituted, and try adding some finely chopped ham.

Pour the milk into a saucepan placed over medium-low heat. When the milk is little more than warm, turn off the heat.

Place a tall, narrow saucepan over low heat. Immediately add 2½ tablespoons of the butter and all of the flour, vigorously stirring them together with a wooden spoon until the butter melts and the flour is incorporated. Once the butter is fully melted, continue cooking and stirring the mixture for a couple of minutes. Then gradually add the warm milk, a little at a time, stirring continuously. Add more milk only after the previously added milk has been fully incorporated. When all the liquid has been added, season to taste with salt and nutmeg and continue to cook, stirring, until thickened, a few minutes longer. Remove from the heat, cover and keep warm.

Place the cauliflower on a rack over gently boiling water. Cover and steam until barely tender, about 10 minutes. Set aside.

Meanwhile, preheat an oven to 350°F (180°C). Grease a 6-by-12-inch (15-by-30-cm) oval baking dish with the remaining 1 tablespoon butter.

Cook your choice of pasta only until half-cooked, then drain. Pour a few spoonfuls of the sauce into the prepared dish. Top with the pasta and then the cauliflower. Pour the remaining sauce over the top. Sprinkle with the cheese. Bake until a golden crust forms on top, about 20 minutes. Serve immediately.

Serves 4

Eggs with Pecorino and Black Pepper
Uova e Pecorino al Pepe

3 eggs
¼ cup (1 oz/30 g) freshly grated
   pecorino cheese
6 tablespoons (3 fl oz/90 ml) milk
freshly ground pepper
½ cup (4 oz/125 g) unsalted butter
salt

Creamy scrambled eggs with cheese form a luscious, rustic sauce for pasta such as fusilli, penne or farfalle, which will hold their shape well during the final stage of cooking in a frying pan. Try substituting Parmesan for the pecorino. Take care not to overcook the eggs, which should remain moist; adding a little of the pasta's cooking water helps.

In a bowl, beat the eggs until well blended. Add the cheese, milk and plenty of pepper and mix together well.

Add your choice of pasta to boiling water. Meanwhile, in a large, wide frying pan over low heat, melt the butter.

When the pasta is almost al dente, drain and add to the frying pan along with the egg mixture and salt to taste. Finish cooking over medium heat, stirring constantly, until the eggs are firm but not dry, 1–2 minutes.

Transfer to a warmed serving dish and serve at once.

Serves 4

Ricotta with Pistachio and Mint

CREMA DI RICOTTA AI PISTACCHI

¼ cup (2 fl oz/60 ml) extra-virgin
  olive oil
¾ cup (6½ oz/200 g) ricotta cheese
salt
freshly ground green peppercorns
⅔ cup (3½ oz/100 g) pistachios,
  coarsely chopped
2 tablespoons chopped fresh mint
  leaves

Light, delicious and refreshing, this topping for cold pasta pairs well with ruote or other round pasta shapes. Substitute hazelnuts (filberts) for the pistachio nuts, if you prefer.

〰

Add your choice of pasta to boiling water. Cook until al dente, then drain, reserving a few tablespoons of the cooking water, and place the pasta in a bowl. Add the olive oil and toss well. Let cool to room temperature, stirring every so often.

While the pasta is cooling, place the ricotta in a bowl, add the reserved hot cooking water and salt and green pepper to taste. Stir until the cheese is smooth and creamy.

When the pasta has cooled, add the ricotta and stir again to coat evenly. Transfer to a serving dish and sprinkle with the nuts and mint. Serve at once. Or, if you like, chill in the refrigerator and sprinkle with the nuts and mint just before serving.

Serves 4

Gorgonzola and Parmesan Cream

CREMA DI GORGONZOLA E PARMIGIANO

2 cups (16 fl oz/500 ml) milk
3½ tablespoons unsalted butter
3½ tablespoons all-purpose (plain) flour
salt
freshly ground pepper
freshly grated nutmeg
¼ lb (120 g) Gorgonzola cheese,
  crumbled
½ cup (2 oz/60 g) freshly grated
  Parmesan cheese

Sharp and tangy, melted Gorgonzola cheese imparts great character to baked pasta dishes featuring rigatoni, gemelli or penne. Take care to season this dish sparingly, as both cheeses are naturally quite salty.

*Pour the milk into a saucepan placed over medium-low heat. When the milk is little more than warm, turn off the heat.

Place a tall, narrow saucepan over low heat. Immediately add 2½ tablespoons of the butter and all of the flour, vigorously stirring them together with a wooden spoon until the butter melts and the flour is incorporated. Once the butter is fully melted, continue cooking and stirring the mixture for a couple of minutes. Then gradually add the warm milk, a little at a time, stirring continuously. Add more milk only after the previously added milk has been fully incorporated with the butter-flour mixture. When all the milk has been added, season to taste with salt, pepper and nutmeg and continue to cook, stirring, until nicely thickened, a few minutes longer. Remove from the heat, cover and keep warm.

Preheat an oven to 350°F (180°C). Grease a 6-by-12-inch (15-by-30-cm) baking dish or 4 small individual baking dishes with the remaining 1 tablespoon butter.

Cook your choice of pasta only until half-cooked, then drain. Transfer to the prepared dish. Add the warm sauce and the Gorgonzola and mix gently. Sprinkle with the Parmesan cheese.

Place in the oven and bake until a golden crust forms on the top, about 20 minutes. Serve immediately.

Serves 4

Curried Omelet and Emmenthaler Cheese

FRITTATINE AL CURRY E FORMAGGIO

2 eggs
2 tablespoons milk
1 tablespoon curry powder
salt
8 tablespoons (4 fl oz/125 ml) extra-
  virgin olive oil
1¼ cups (6½ oz/200 g) shelled peas
5 oz (155 g) Emmenthaler or mozzarella
  cheese, cut into ⅓-inch (1-cm) cubes
2 tablespoons chopped fresh flat-leaf
  (Italian) parsley
freshly ground pepper

A hint of curry flavors strips of omelet tossed with cheese and peas in this summertime dish. Use fusilli, shells or other pasta shapes that will hold up well when cooled. For a heartier version, add 3½ ounces (100 g) diced cooked ham with the cheese.

𝄞

In a bowl and using a fork, beat together 1 of the eggs, 1 table-spoon of the milk, ½ tablespoon of the curry powder and salt to taste until smooth and creamy. In a nonstick frying pan over medium heat, warm 1 tablespoon of the olive oil. Pour in the beaten egg mixture to form a very thin omelet. Cook until the bottom is set, about 1 minute. Using a flat pan cover or plate, turn the omelet out of the pan and then slip it back into the pan, browned side up. Cook until the second side is firm, about 30 seconds longer. Transfer to a flat surface to cool. When cool, roll it up into a loose cylinder and slice crosswise into thin strips. Make a second omelet in the same way with the remaining egg, milk and curry powder, salt to taste and 1 tablespoon oil. Roll and cut into thin strips. Set aside.

Bring the water for cooking the pasta to a boil and add the peas. When the water returns to the boil, add your choice of pasta. Cook until al dente, drain the pasta and peas and place in a bowl. Add 2 tablespoons of the olive oil and toss well. Let cool to room temperature, stirring every so often.

Transfer to a serving dish and add the cheese, omelet strips, the remaining 4 tablespoons (2 fl oz/60 ml) oil and the parsley. Toss well and season to taste with pepper. Serve at once, or chill for 1 hour before serving.

Serves 4

Artichokes and Mozzarella
CARCIOFI E MOZZARELLA

juice of 1 lemon
6 artichokes, about 3 oz (90 g) each
6 tablespoons (3 fl oz/90 ml) extra-
  virgin olive oil
2 small cloves garlic, finely chopped
6 oz (185 g) mozzarella cheese, cut into
  small cubes
3 tablespoons chopped fresh mint
  leaves
salt
freshly ground pepper

Sautéed artichoke hearts make a delectable, easy topping for penne or gemelli. Other vegetables can be used, including fennel, Belgian endive and radicchio—all sliced and sautéed in the same manner as the artichokes.

∭

Have ready a bowl of water three-fourths full to which you have added the lemon juice. Remove the stem and tough outer leaves from the artichokes until you reach the pale green heart. Cut each artichoke in half lengthwise. Scoop out the prickly choke from the center and discard. Cut the artichokes lengthwise into long, thin slices. As the artichokes are cut, place them in the bowl of water.

In a large frying pan over medium heat, warm the olive oil. Add the garlic, reduce the heat to very low and cook very slowly until the garlic takes on its distinctive golden color without burning, about 5 minutes.

Drain the artichokes, pat them dry and add to the frying pan. Raise the heat to medium and sauté, stirring often, until the artichokes are tender, 5–6 minutes. Remove from the heat and add the mozzarella.

Meanwhile, cook your choice of pasta until al dente. Drain and transfer to a warmed serving dish. Immediately add the contents of the frying pan, the mint and salt and pepper to taste. Toss well; the warmth of the pasta will melt the cheese. Serve at once.

Serves 4

Emmenthaler Cheese and Onion

EMMENTHAL E CIPOLLE

¼ cup (2 oz/60 g) plus 1 tablespoon
  unsalted butter

1¼ lb (600 g) white onions, very
  thinly sliced

salt

freshly ground pepper

2 bay leaves

½ cup (4 fl oz/125 ml) milk

½ cup (4 fl oz/125 ml) vegetable stock

1 cup (4 oz/120 g) grated Emmenthaler
  cheese

Lightly spiced with bay leaves, this sauce is ideal for preparing a broiler-browned gratin with pasta ribbons of any size. Other Swiss-type cheeses such as Gruyère or Jarlsberg may replace the Emmenthaler, or use slices of mozzarella. If you like, add ¼ pound (120 g) cooked ham, cut into small dice, to the sauce once the liquids have been absorbed.

∭

*I*n a saucepan over medium heat, melt the ¼ cup (2 oz/ 60 g) butter. Add the onions and sauté for a couple of minutes. Stir in salt and pepper to taste and the bay leaves. Add the milk and stock, reduce the heat to low and simmer uncovered, stirring occasionally, until the liquids are absorbed, about 30 minutes. Discard the bay leaves.

  Meanwhile, preheat a broiler (griller). Grease a 6-by-12-inch (15-by-30-cm) flameproof dish with the 1 tablespoon butter.

  Cook your choice of pasta until al dente. Drain and immediately place in the prepared dish. Spoon the hot onion sauce evenly over the top, then top with the cheese.

  Place the dish under the broiler and broil (grill) until the top is golden, about 5 minutes. Serve immediately.

Serves 4

Eggs with Leeks and Cream
CREMA DI UOVA AI PORRI

10 oz (300 g) leeks
¼ cup (2 oz/60 g) unsalted butter
4 eggs
1 cup (4 oz/120 g) freshly grated
   Parmesan cheese
¼ cup (2 fl oz/60 ml) light (single)
   cream
salt
freshly ground pepper

All this vegetarian recipe lacks to become a traditional carbonara sauce is the addition of ¼ pound (120 g) bacon, chopped and sautéed with the leeks. That heartier version goes well with spaghetti; this more delicate sauce is best served with fine strands such as angel hair, and is also good with penne or gemelli. Cook the pasta until almost al dente, since it will continue cooking with the sauce in the frying pan.

ʃʃʃʃ

Trim the leeks, discarding the root ends and the tough green tops. Slit the leeks lengthwise three-fourths of the way down to the root ends. Wash under cold running water to remove all dirt. Cut the white portions and the tender green tops crosswise into very thin slices.

In a large, wide frying pan over medium heat, melt the butter. Add the leeks and sauté, stirring, until tender, about 5 minutes. Remove from the heat, cover and keep warm.

In a bowl, beat together the eggs, ¼ cup (1 oz/30 g) of the Parmesan cheese, the cream and salt and pepper to taste. Set aside.

Cook your choice of pasta until almost al dente. Drain the pasta, add it to the frying pan holding the leeks and raise the heat to high. Pour in the egg mixture and stir vigorously until the eggs are firm but not dry, 1–2 minutes.

Transfer to a warmed serving dish and serve immediately. Pass the remaining ¾ cup (3 oz/90 g) Parmesan cheese at the table.

Serves 4

Trout and Tomatoes with Hard-Cooked Eggs
TROTA AFFUMICATA, POMODORI E UOVA SODE

3 ripe tomatoes, about ½ lb (240 g) total weight
coarse salt
6½ oz (200 g) green beans, trimmed
4 tablespoons (2 fl oz/60 ml) extra-virgin olive oil
8 oz (250 g) boned smoked trout, broken into small pieces
2 tablespoons well-drained capers
8 fresh basil leaves, torn into small pieces
2 hard-cooked eggs, thinly sliced crosswise
12 black olives such as Niçoise

Tasty and colorful, this topping for cold pasta is ideal with large shells, which not only look attractive but also stay al dente once they have cooled. If you'd like the pasta chilled, place in the refrigerator for up to 1 hour before serving.

*P*eel the tomatoes and chop them into small cubes. Place in a sieve, sprinkle with coarse salt and let stand for 30 minutes to drain off excess liquid.

Meanwhile, fill a saucepan three-fourths full of water. Bring to a boil, add coarse salt to taste and the green beans and boil until tender, about 5 minutes. Drain into a colander, place under cold running water and drain again. Cut the beans on the diagonal into ¾-inch (2-cm) lengths. Set aside.

Cook your choice of pasta until al dente. Drain and transfer to a large serving bowl. Add 2 tablespoons of the olive oil and mix well. Let cool to room temperature, stirring every so often.

Add the trout, tomatoes, green beans, capers, basil and the remaining 2 tablespoons olive oil to the cooled pasta. Toss well. Decorate with the egg slices and olives and serve.

Serves 4

Salmon and Caviar Cream
Crema di Salmone e Caviale

½ cup (4 fl oz/125 ml) heavy (double)
  cream
¼ cup (2 oz/60 g) unsalted butter
8 oz (250 g) salmon fillet, sliced
  paper-thin on the diagonal
salt
freshly ground white pepper
3 tablespoons caviar

Quick and elegant, this mixture goes perfectly with tagliatelle or fettuccine. Use any type of roe that you like. For extra flavor, use smoked salmon instead of the fresh fish. To make a more complex-tasting, less costly variation, substitute a heaping tablespoon of whole fennel seeds for the caviar, adding them to the cream with the salmon.

Add your choice of pasta to boiling water. While it cooks, combine the cream and butter in a saucepan over low heat. Bring to a boil very slowly. Remove from the heat as soon as the cream boils. Add the salmon and salt and white pepper to taste. Mix well.

When the pasta is al dente, drain and transfer to a warmed serving dish. Immediately pour the sauce over the pasta, sprinkle on the caviar and serve at once.

Serves 4

Tuna with Mint and Capers

TONNO MENTA E CAPPERI

3 plum (Roma) tomatoes
coarse salt
1 lb (500 g) canned tuna in olive oil,
  flaked and chopped
6 tablespoons (3 oz/90 g) well-drained
  capers
18 fresh mint leaves
1½ teaspoons fresh lemon juice
6 tablespoons (3 fl oz/90 ml) extra-
  virgin olive oil
regular salt
cayenne pepper

A refreshing spur-of-the-moment sauce for a hot day, this recipe requires no cooking. Serve with farfalle, shells or similar pasta shapes. If you like, add some finely chopped green (spring) onion.

Peel the tomatoes and chop them into small cubes. Place in a sieve, sprinkle with coarse salt and let stand for 30 minutes to drain off excess liquid.

Place the tuna in a bowl. On a chopping board, combine the capers and mint and chop together finely. Add to the tuna. Sprinkle with the lemon juice and stir to mix well. Add the tomatoes and 3 tablespoons of the olive oil. Season to taste with regular salt and cayenne pepper. Allow to stand at room temperature for 10 minutes, so the flavors mingle.

Meanwhile, cook your choice of pasta until al dente. Drain, place in a bowl and toss with the remaining 3 table-spoons olive oil. Let cool to room temperature, stirring every so often.

Add the tuna mixture to the cooled pasta and toss well. Transfer to a serving dish and serve.

Serves 4

Scallops and Tomatoes
CAPESANTE E POMODORI

12 sea scallops

6 tablespoons (3 fl oz/90 ml) extra-virgin olive oil

2 small cloves garlic, thinly sliced

3 or 4 plum (Roma) tomatoes, peeled and chopped

salt

freshly ground pepper

3 tablespoons chopped fresh basil

Select the fullest-flavored vine-ripened plum tomatoes in the market. Buy the freshest scallops you can find; their sweet, mild flavor will be highlighted by the ripe, barely cooked tomatoes. Circular pasta shapes look nice with the scallops.

*C*ut the scallops into rounds ¼ inch (6 mm) thick. Set aside.

Add your choice of pasta to boiling water. When the pasta is half-cooked, warm the olive oil in a large frying pan over medium heat. Add the garlic and sauté until it starts to brown, a couple of minutes. Raise the heat to high and add the scallops and tomatoes. Cook, stirring gently, until the scallops are opaque, 1–2 minutes. Season to taste with salt and pepper.

When the pasta is al dente, drain and transfer to a warmed serving dish. Pour the scallop sauce over the pasta; toss well. Sprinkle with the basil and serve immediately.

Serves 4

Anchovies with Zucchini and Capers
ACCIUGHE, ZUCCHINI E CAPPERI

¼ cup (2 fl oz/60 ml) extra-virgin
   olive oil
3 cloves garlic, sliced
4 small zucchini (courgettes), trimmed
   and cut into ⅓-inch (9-mm) cubes
2 tablespoons well-drained capers
8 anchovy fillets in olive oil, drained
   and cut into small pieces
1 tablespoon dried oregano
salt
freshly ground pepper

The pronounced, salty taste of anchovies and capers is tempered somewhat by zucchini in a casual sauce ideal with spaghetti. Choose small zucchini, which have a better flavor. Grated cheese is not normally served with this sauce. Instead, fry bread crumbs in a little olive oil until golden and pass at the table. For a spicier effect, add a pinch of cayenne pepper to the crumbs while they fry.

In a large, wide frying pan over medium heat, warm the olive oil. Add the garlic and sauté, stirring, until crisp, about 3 minutes. Add the zucchini, capers, anchovies, oregano and salt and pepper to taste. (Remember, anchovies are salty, so be cautious when adding salt.) Sauté over high heat until the zucchini are just tender, about 4 minutes.

Meanwhile, cook your choice of pasta until almost al dente. Drain, reserving about ¼ cup (2 fl oz/60 ml) of the cooking water. Add the pasta and reserved hot cooking water to the frying pan with the sauce and finish cooking over high heat, stirring constantly, for 1–2 minutes.

Transfer to a warmed serving dish; serve immediately.

Serves 4

Mussels with Cannellini Cream
CREMA DI COZZE E FAGIOLI

⅔ cup (5 oz/155 g) dried cannellini, small white (navy) or Great Northern beans

2 lb (1 kg) mussels in the shell, well scrubbed and debearded

salt

freshly ground pepper

6 tablespoons (3 fl oz/90 ml) extra-virgin olive oil

2 cloves garlic, sliced

10 fresh sage leaves

This sauce is ideal for wide pasta ribbons such as pappardelle. For the best results, buy mussels only from the most reputable fish-mongers, and only at their peak of season; do not make this during warmer months, when mussels are chancy.

*P*lace the beans in a bowl, add water to cover and soak for 12 hours at room temperature, changing the water a few times.

Drain the beans and place in a saucepan. Add water to cover by 1 inch (2.5 cm). Bring to a boil, reduce the heat to low, cover partially and cook until completely tender, at least 1½ hours.

Drain the beans, reserving the cooking liquid. Transfer to a food processor fitted with the metal blade or to a blender. Process until creamy, adding cooking liquid if needed. Set aside.

Place the mussels in a saucepan. Cover and place over medium heat until the mussels open, a few minutes. Discard any that do not open. Using a slotted spoon, transfer the mussels to a bowl. Strain the liquid in the pan through a fine-mesh sieve; set aside. Remove the mussels from their shells and discard the shells. Combine the mussels, puréed beans and salt and pepper to taste in a frying pan over medium heat. Stir to prevent sticking and add the mussel liquid as needed for moisture. Keep hot.

In a saucepan over medium heat, warm the olive oil. Add the garlic and sage, reduce the heat to very low and cook until the leaves are crisp and the garlic is golden, about 5 minutes. Using a slotted spoon, transfer the sage to a small dish.

Meanwhile, cook your choice of pasta until al dente. Drain and transfer to a warmed serving dish. Pour on the hot garlic and oil and toss well. Top with the bean-mussel mixture and garnish with the sage. Sprinkle with pepper and serve.

Serves 4

Clams with Garlic and Parsley

SALSA ALLE VONGOLE

1½ lb (750 g) clams in the shell, well
  scrubbed
6 tablespoons (3 fl oz/90 ml) extra-
  virgin olive oil
3 cloves garlic, sliced
3 tablespoons minced fresh flat-leaf
  (Italian) parsley

Always use fresh clams, still in the shell, for the most traditional rendition of this favorite sauce for spaghetti or bucatini. Place one or more plates on the dining table for collecting the discarded shells. To rid the clams of their grit, soak them in a large quantity of water for several hours before cooking.

Place the clams in a large saucepan, discarding any that do not close when you touch them. Cover and place over medium heat. In a few minutes the clams will open and release their juice. Discard any that do not open. Remove from the heat. Using a slotted spoon, transfer the clams to a bowl. Strain the liquid in the pan through a fine-mesh sieve to remove any sand or grit. There should be about ½ cup (4 fl oz/125 ml) liquid. Set aside.

Add your choice of pasta to boiling water. When it is half-cooked, warm the olive oil in a large, wide frying pan over medium heat. Add the garlic and sauté, stirring, until crisp, about 3 minutes.

When the pasta is almost al dente, drain and add to the frying pan with the garlic. Add the clams, the strained liquid and parsley and finish cooking over high heat, stirring constantly, for 1–2 minutes.

Transfer to a warmed serving dish; serve immediately.

Serves 4

Shrimp and Fennel with Lemon Zest

GAMBERETTI E FINOCCHIO AL PROFUMO DI LIMONE

The mild anise flavor of the fennel and the tartness of the lemon zest enhance the natural sweetness of fresh shrimp. Serve with taglierini, tagliatelle or angel hair pasta, or, for a change, ruote or a similar shape. For a stronger fennel flavor, substitute 2 tablespoons fennel seeds for the parsley, adding them during the final moments of cooking.

6 tablespoons (3 fl oz/90 ml) extra-virgin olive oil

2 fennel bulbs, trimmed and cut crosswise into paper-thin slices

6 tablespoons (3 fl oz/90 ml) dry white wine

1 lb (500 g) medium-sized shrimp (prawns), peeled and deveined

salt

pinch of cayenne pepper

1½ tablespoons grated lemon zest

1½ tablespoons chopped fresh flat-leaf (Italian) parsley

*I*n a large, wide frying pan over medium heat, warm the olive oil. Raise the heat to high and add the fennel. Sauté, stirring, for about 2 minutes. Add the white wine and cook until the wine evaporates, just a few minutes longer. Add the shrimp and salt and cayenne pepper to taste and continue to cook over high heat, stirring constantly, until the shrimp turn pink and curl and the fennel is tender, a couple of minutes longer.

Meanwhile, cook your choice of pasta until almost al dente. Drain, reserving about ½ cup (4 fl oz/125 ml) of the cooking water. Add the pasta and lemon zest to the sauce in the frying pan and finish cooking over high heat, stirring constantly and adding the reserved hot cooking water if needed to moisten, for 1–2 minutes.

Transfer to a warmed serving dish, sprinkle with the parsley and serve.

Serves 4

Tuna, Tomatoes and Mushrooms

TONNO, POMODORI E FUNGHI

8 tablespoons (4 fl oz/125 ml) extra-virgin olive oil

2 cloves garlic

1 small dried red chili pepper

¾ lb (375 g) plum (Roma) tomatoes, peeled and chopped

2 tablespoons minced fresh basil

pinch of salt

4 oz (120 g) canned tuna in olive oil, drained and finely flaked

2 anchovy fillets in olive oil, drained and cut into small pieces

3 oz (90 g) fresh shiitake mushrooms, stemmed and cut into ¾-inch (2-cm) cubes

freshly ground pepper

Rich and flavorful, this meaty-tasting sauce marries well with long, flattened strands like linguine or bucatini. A more traditional alternative to the steaklike shiitake mushrooms would be fresh porcini.

In a large, wide frying pan over medium heat, warm 3 tablespoons of the olive oil. Add the garlic cloves and chili pepper and sauté, stirring, for a couple of minutes. Add the tomatoes, basil and salt and cook uncovered, stirring often, until creamy but not too dry, about 15 minutes. Discard the garlic cloves and chili pepper.

While the tomatoes are cooking, warm 3 tablespoons of the olive oil in another frying pan over medium heat. Add the tuna, anchovies and mushrooms. Raise the heat to high and cook, stirring, for a couple of minutes.

Cook your choice of pasta until al dente. Drain and transfer to a warmed serving platter, toss with the remaining 2 tablespoons olive oil and pepper to taste. Spoon the two sauces in alternating vertical stripes atop the pasta. Serve at once.

Serves 4

Smoked Salmon with Radicchio

SALMONE AFFUMICATO E RADICCHIO

¼ cup (2 oz/60 g) unsalted butter
½ white onion, thinly sliced crosswise
3–4 tablespoons water
½ lb (250 g) radicchio, cut into thin
   strips
¼ cup (2 fl oz/60 ml) dry white wine
salt
freshly ground white pepper
3½ oz (100 g) smoked salmon, cut into
   strips
2 tablespoons chopped fresh flat-leaf
   (Italian) parsley

Delicate and elegant, this combination goes best with linguine, taglierini, fusilli or fresh egg tagliatelle.

◎

*I*n a large frying pan over medium heat, melt the butter. Add the onion and water, cover and cook gently, stirring occasionally, until tender and translucent, about 10 minutes.

Add the radicchio, white wine and salt and white pepper to taste. Stir well, raise the heat to high and cook until the wine evaporates, a few minutes.

As soon as the wine has evaporated, add the salmon and continue sautéing until heated through.

Meanwhile, cook your choice of pasta until almost al dente. Drain, reserving about ¼ cup (2 fl oz/60 ml) of the cooking water. Add the pasta and the reserved hot cooking water to the radicchio sauce in the pan. Finish cooking over high heat, stirring constantly, for 1–2 minutes.

Transfer to a warmed serving dish, sprinkle with the parsley and serve immediately.

Serves 4

Shrimp and Eggplant
GAMBERETTI E MELANZANE

½ cup (4 fl oz/125 ml) extra-virgin
  olive oil
1 white or red (Spanish) onion, coarsely
  chopped
2 small cloves garlic, finely chopped
3 slender (Asian) eggplants (aubergines),
  about 6 oz (185 g) each, trimmed and
  cut into small cubes
18 shrimp (prawns), peeled and
  deveined
1½ tablespoons small fresh thyme
  leaves
salt

A fairly quick sauté, this seafood topping is also good made with clams or mussels. If you can't find slender Asian eggplants, use the smallest globe eggplants available. The sauce is perfect with penne, or try it with other medium-sized pasta shapes such as fusilli and farfalle.

In a large, wide frying pan over medium heat, warm the olive oil. Add the onion and garlic and sauté, stirring, for a couple of minutes. Add the eggplant and continue sautéing, stirring often, until tender, about 15 minutes.

Meanwhile, cook your choice of pasta until al dente. A few minutes before it is ready, add the shrimp to the eggplant and cook, stirring, until they curl and turn pink, 3–4 minutes.

Drain the pasta and transfer to a warmed serving dish. Immediately pour the sauce over the pasta, add the thyme and salt to taste and toss well. Serve at once.

Serves 4

Chicken and Pistachios with Marsala and Lemon Zest

POLLO E PISTACCHI

8 tablespoons (4 oz/125 g) unsalted butter

3 tablespoons chopped white onion

2 tablespoons water

6 oz (185 g) boned and skinned chicken breast, cut into thin strips

2 tablespoons dry Marsala

2 tablespoons finely shredded lemon zest

¾ cup (3 oz/90 g) pistachios, coarsely chopped

5 oz (155 g) fairly stale coarse country bread, crusts discarded and bread crumbled

salt

Thin strips of chicken breast take on great delicacy when combined with the other ingredients in this wonderful topping for linguine or pappardelle. If you like, substitute walnuts and Cognac for the pistachios and Marsala.

⁂

*I*n a frying pan over low heat, melt 3 tablespoons of the butter. Add the onion and the water, cover and cook gently, stirring occasionally, until tender and completely translucent, about 10 minutes. Add the chicken, raise the heat to high and sauté, stirring often, until almost cooked through, 7–8 minutes.

Reduce the heat, add the Marsala, 2 tablespoons of the butter, the lemon zest and pistachios. Stir well and simmer, stirring occasionally, for another couple of minutes. Remove from the heat, cover and keep warm.

In a small frying pan over medium heat, melt the remaining 3 tablespoons butter. Add the bread crumbs and a little salt, raise the heat to high and toast, stirring often, until they turn golden, a couple of minutes.

Meanwhile, cook your choice of pasta until al dente. Drain and transfer to a warmed serving dish. Immediately pour the sauce over the pasta and toss well. Sprinkle with the hot bread crumbs and serve at once.

Serves 4

Salami, Mozzarella and Tomatoes

SALAME, MOZZARELLA E POMODORINI

6 tablespoons (3 fl oz/90 ml) extra-virgin olive oil

8 small cherry tomatoes, cut in half

4 oz (125 g) salami, diced

2 celery stalks, trimmed and thinly sliced

1 yellow, red or green bell pepper (capsicum), seeded, deribbed and cut into thin strips

4 oz (125 g) mozzarella cheese, diced

salt

freshly ground white pepper

2 tablespoons minced fresh oregano

In this cold, uncooked topping for elbow macaroni, the powerful flavor of Italian salami is tamed by bell peppers, celery and perfectly ripe cherry tomatoes. Serve on a bed of tender young lettuces for an attractive presentation.

Cook your choice of pasta until al dente. Drain and transfer to a bowl. Add 2 tablespoons of the olive oil and toss well. Let cool to room temperature, stirring every so often.

Add the remaining 4 tablespoons (2 fl oz/60 ml) olive oil, the cherry tomatoes, salami, celery, bell pepper, mozzarella and salt and white pepper to taste. Toss well, sprinkle with the oregano and toss again. Serve at once. Or, if you like, cover and refrigerate until well chilled before serving.

Serve 4

Prosciutto and Porcini with Red Wine

PROSCIUTTO E PORCINI AL VINO ROSSO

3 oz (90 g) sliced prosciutto

5 tablespoons (2½ oz/75 g) unsalted
   butter, at room temperature

2 tablespoons chopped white onion

3 oz (90 g) fresh porcini mushrooms,
   sliced

10 oz (300 g) ripe plum (Roma)
   tomatoes, peeled and chopped

6 fresh basil leaves, coarsely chopped

salt

freshly ground pepper

⅔ cup (5 fl oz/150 ml) dry red wine

¾ cup (3 oz/90 g) freshly grated
   Parmesan cheese

Emphatically rich, this sauce goes well with robust pasta shapes such as plain or spinach armoniche or rigatoni. An even heartier version calls for adding 3 ounces (90 g) chicken livers, coarsely chopped, and browns them with the mushrooms. Replace the porcini with any full-flavored wild or domestic mushrooms.

*T*rim the fat from the prosciutto slices and reserve. Cut the lean portion into thin strips.

In a frying pan over low heat, combine the prosciutto fat, 1 tablespoon of the butter and the onion. Sauté slowly, stirring occasionally, until the onion is browned, about 10 minutes. Add the lean prosciutto and mushrooms and continue to sauté, stirring, for a couple of minutes. Add the tomatoes, basil and salt and pepper to taste and simmer uncovered, stirring every so often, until the liquid evaporates and the sauce is slightly thickened and creamy, about 15 minutes longer.

Meanwhile, in a small saucepan, simmer the red wine until it is reduced by half. Add the wine to the sauce. Continue to simmer until the wine almost totally evaporates, then remove from the heat, cover and keep warm.

When the sauce is nearly ready, add your choice of pasta to boiling water. When the pasta is al dente, drain and transfer to a warmed serving dish. Immediately add the remaining 4 tablespoons (2 oz/60 g) butter and toss well. Top the pasta with the sauce and serve at once. Pass the Parmesan cheese at the table.

Serves 4

Ham and Spinach with Cream
PROSCIUTTO E SPINACI

1 lb (500 g) spinach, trimmed,
   thoroughly washed and leaves torn
   into pieces
¼ cup (2 oz/60 g) unsalted butter
3 oz (90 g) cooked ham, cut into thin
   strips
6 tablespoons (3 fl oz/90 ml) heavy
   (double) cream
freshly grated nutmeg
salt
¾ cup (3 oz/90 g) freshly grated
   Parmesan cheese

The simple union of fresh spinach, ham and a splash of cream makes an excellent topping for regular or green taglierini or tagliatelle. Steaming rather than boiling the spinach gives it more flavor and a better texture.

*B*ring a saucepan three-fourths full of water to a boil. Add the spinach and boil until tender, about 2 minutes. Alternatively, place the spinach in a steamer rack over gently boiling water, cover and steam until tender, 3–4 minutes. Drain well, press out all the excess water and then chop the spinach.

   In a frying pan over medium heat, melt the butter. Add the spinach and sauté until all moisture evaporates, a few minutes. Add the ham, cream and a generous grating of nutmeg and cook, stirring constantly, a couple of minutes longer. Season to taste with salt.

   Meanwhile, cook your choice of pasta until al dente. Drain and transfer to a warmed serving dish. Immediately pour the sauce over the pasta and toss very gently. Sprinkle with ¼ cup (1 oz/30 g) of the Parmesan cheese and serve at once. Pass the remaining Parmesan at the table.

Serves 4

Sausage and Swiss Chard
SALSICCIA E BIETOLE

6 tablespoons (3 fl oz/90 ml) extra-
   virgin olive oil
2 cloves garlic, minced
6 oz (185 g) Italian sweet sausage,
   casings removed and meat crumbled
1 bunch Swiss chard, about 1 lb
   (500 g), stalks removed and green
   leaves cut into thin strips
½ cup (2 oz/60 g) freshly grated
   pecorino cheese

The flavor of the Swiss chard nicely counterbalances the richness of the sausage in this quick sauté for tossing with pappardelle or linguine. For a sweet-and-sour accent, add 2 tablespoons raisins—soaked in warm water to cover until soft, drained and then patted dry—to the frying pan with the pasta.

In a large, wide frying pan over medium heat, warm 2 tablespoons of the olive oil. Add the garlic, reduce the heat to very low and cook very slowly, stirring, so the garlic takes on its distinctive golden color without burning, about 5 minutes. Add the sausage and continue to cook, stirring, until cooked but not browned, a couple of minutes. Remove from the heat, cover and keep warm.

Bring the water for cooking the pasta to a boil. Add the Swiss chard. When the water returns to a boil, add your choice of pasta as well and cook until almost al dente. Drain the pasta and Swiss chard and add to the frying pan with the sausage. Finish cooking over high heat, stirring constantly, for 1–2 minutes.

Transfer to a warmed serving dish. Immediately add the pecorino cheese and the remaining 4 tablespoons (2 fl oz/ 60 ml) oil and toss well. Serve at once.

Serves 4

Tomatoes and Bacon
PUTTANESCA

2 tablespoons extra-virgin olive oil

3 oz (80 g) bacon, cut into squares

10 oz (300 g) fresh plum (Roma) tomatoes, peeled, seeded and chopped, or canned plum tomatoes, drained and chopped

2 pinches of cayenne pepper

salt

This popular combination of bacon and tomatoes is named in Italy for the ladies of easy virtue who reputedly invented it. It can be spiced with as much cayenne pepper as you like. Eat it hot when the weather is cold, or at cool room temperature when the sun is hot. Puttanesca sauce is traditionally paired with spaghetti, but feel free to toss it with your favorite pasta shape.

*I*n a frying pan over medium heat, warm the olive oil. Add the bacon and fry until crisp, about 5 minutes. Add the tomatoes, cayenne pepper and salt to taste. Raise the heat to high and sauté, stirring occasionally, until the sauce thickens, about 10 minutes.

Meanwhile, cook your choice of pasta until al dente. Drain and transfer to a warmed serving dish. Immediately pour the sauce over the pasta and toss well. Serve at once.

Serves 4

Chicken with Eggplant and Button Mushrooms

POLLO, MELANZANE E FUNGHI

6 tablespoons (3 fl oz/90 ml) extra-virgin olive oil

3 cloves garlic, sliced

2 small slender (Asian) eggplants (aubergines), ½ lb (250 g) total weight, cut into tiny cubes

¾ lb (375 g) boned and skinned chicken breast, cut into ¾-inch (2-cm) cubes

6 oz (185 g) very small fresh button mushrooms

1½ tablespoons dried oregano

salt

freshly ground pepper

1 cup (4 oz/125 g) freshly grated Parmesan cheese

This rapid sauté of autumnal ingredients makes an ideal quick topping for bucatini or other pasta strands. If you can't find slender Asian eggplants, substitute the smallest globe eggplants available. Lean pork can stand in for the chicken.

In a frying pan over low heat, warm the olive oil. Add the garlic and sauté, stirring, until crisp, about 3 minutes. Add the eggplant, chicken and mushrooms, raise the heat to medium and cook, stirring often, until the vegetables are tender and the chicken is cooked, about 10 minutes. Add the oregano and season to taste with salt and pepper. Remove from the heat, cover and keep warm.

Meanwhile, cook your choice of pasta until al dente. Drain and transfer to a warmed serving dish. Immediately pour the sauce over the pasta, toss well and serve at once. Pass the Parmesan cheese at the table.

Serves 4

Curried Chicken with Broccoli and Raisins

POLLO E BROCCOLI AL CURRY

1¼ lb (625 g) broccoli

6 tablespoons (3 oz/90 g) unsalted butter

3 tablespoons chopped white onion

1½ tablespoons water

½ lb (250 g) boned and skinned chicken breast, cut into thin strips

6 tablespoons (2½ oz/75 g) raisins, soaked in warm water to cover for 30 minutes and drained

3 tablespoons curry powder, dissolved in 6 tablespoons (3 fl oz/90 ml) light (single) cream

salt

If you like your food particularly spicy, increase the amount of curry powder. Take some care, though, because the strength of curry powders varies with the brand and the particular blend. Try this sauce on either tagliatelle or pappardelle. Lean, tender lamb may be substituted for the chicken.

❖

Cut the broccoli stalks from the florets. Peel the stalks and slice them crosswise ⅓ inch (1 cm) thick. Divide the tops into florets about 1 inch (2.5 cm) in diameter. Set aside.

In a large, wide frying pan over medium heat, melt the butter. Add the onion and water, cover and cook gently, stirring occasionally, until tender and completely translucent, about 10 minutes. Uncover and add the chicken, raisins and the curry powder–cream mixture and continue cooking, stirring occasionally, until the sauce is reduced and the chicken is cooked through, 7–8 minutes. Remove from the heat, cover and keep warm.

Bring the water for cooking the pasta to a boil. Add salt to taste and the broccoli florets and stalk slices. When the water returns to a boil, add your choice of pasta as well. Cook until al dente, drain the pasta and broccoli and transfer to a warmed serving dish. Immediately pour the warm sauce over the pasta and serve at once.

Serves 4

Bacon and Provolone
Pancetta e Provolone

2 tablespoons extra-virgin olive oil

6 oz (185 g) pancetta or bacon, cut into thin strips

3 tablespoons finely chopped white onion

5 very ripe plum (Roma) tomatoes, peeled and coarsely chopped

salt

pinch of cayenne pepper

¾ cup (3 oz/90 g) grated provolone cheese

A classic Italian all'amatriciana *sauce for spaghetti is subtly altered here by substituting rich, tangy provolone for the traditional pecorino cheese. For a somewhat lighter version, omit the olive oil and sauté the pancetta or bacon with the onion in a nonstick pan; you can even omit the cheese, adding a little more cayenne pepper for extra flavor.*

*I*n a frying pan over medium heat, warm the olive oil. Add the pancetta or bacon and fry until crisp, about 5 minutes. Using a slotted spoon, transfer to a small bowl; set aside.

Add the onion to the pan and sauté, stirring, until tender, 3–5 minutes. Add the tomatoes and salt and cayenne pepper to taste. Cook uncovered, stirring occasionally, until the liquid evaporates and the sauce is slightly thickened and creamy, about 10 minutes.

Meanwhile, cook your choice of pasta until al dente. Drain and transfer to a warmed serving dish. Immediately pour the hot sauce over the pasta, add the provolone and pancetta or bacon and toss well. Serve at once.

Serves 4

Bolognese Meat Sauce
RAGÙ ALLA BOLOGNESE

3 tablespoons unsalted butter

2 tablespoons extra-virgin olive oil

1 small carrot, peeled and finely chopped

1 celery stalk, trimmed and finely chopped

1 small white onion, finely chopped

½ lb (240 g) ground (minced) beef

1 tablespoon fresh flat-leaf (Italian) parsley

2 oz (50 g) dried porcini mushrooms, preferably in slices, soaked in warm water to cover for 20 minutes and drained

¼ cup (2 fl oz/60 ml) dry white wine

3 plum (Roma) tomatoes, peeled, seeded and chopped

salt

freshly ground pepper

freshly grated nutmeg

1 cup (8 fl oz/250 ml) water

¾ cup (3 oz/90 g) freshly grated Parmesan cheese

The product of slow, patient simmering for at least an hour, this well-known meat sauce from Bologna has a rich, full flavor that complements any fresh or dried pasta, but especially spaghetti, fettuccine, ravioli and tagliatelle. Although it is traditionally cooked in earthenware to prevent sticking, any heavy-bottomed or nonstick pan can be used. The secret behind the sauce's complex taste lies in cooking the vegetables to the point where they almost—but not quite—burn. The addition of chopped chicken livers, sausage or ground pork will result in an even more elaborate sauce. For a more elegant presentation, toss the cooked pasta with ⅓ cup (3 oz/90 g) unsalted butter and serve the sauce from a bowl alongside.

In a large frying pan over medium heat, melt the butter with the olive oil. Add the carrot, celery and onion and cook, stirring, until very tender, 20 minutes or longer.

Add the beef and parsley and raise the heat to high. Cook, stirring often, for 3–4 minutes. If the mushrooms are not already in slices, slice them. Add the mushrooms and white wine to the frying pan and continue cooking and stirring a few minutes longer to evaporate the wine. Add the tomatoes and reduce the heat to low. Stir in salt and pepper to taste and a grating of nutmeg. Pour in the water, stir well, cover and simmer until the the sauce reduces considerably and is very thick, at least 1 hour longer.

When the sauce is ready, cook your choice of pasta until al dente. Drain and transfer to a warmed serving dish. Immediately pour the sauce over the pasta and toss well. Pass the Parmesan cheese at the table.

Serves 4

Ham and Peas

PROSCIUTTO E PISELLI

2 cups (16 fl oz/500 ml) milk
3½ tablespoons unsalted butter
3½ tablespoons all-purpose (plain) flour
1 tablespoon chopped fresh tarragon
¼ lb (120 g) cooked ham, sliced and
   then cut into ⅓-inch (1-cm) squares
salt
1¼ cups (6½ oz/200 g) shelled peas
½ cup (2 oz/60 g) freshly grated
   Parmesan cheese

Dotted with strips of ham and fresh green peas, a flour-and-butter–thickened sauce binds this baked pasta dish. Penne or rigatoni are ideal shapes to use. If you like, replace the tarragon with a pinch of freshly grated nutmeg.

⁙•

Pour the milk into a saucepan placed over medium-low heat. When the milk is little more than warm, turn off the heat.

Place a tall, narrow saucepan over low heat. Immediately add 2½ tablespoons of the butter and all of the flour, vigorously stirring them together with a wooden spoon until the butter melts and the flour is incorporated. Once the butter is fully melted, continue cooking and stirring the mixture for a couple of minutes. Then gradually add the warm milk, a little at a time, stirring continuously. Add more milk only after the previously added milk has been fully incorporated. When all the milk has been added, cook, stirring, until thickened, a few minutes longer. Add the tarragon, ham and salt to taste and stir a few seconds longer. Remove from the heat, cover and keep warm.

Preheat a broiler (griller). Grease a 6-by-12-inch (15-by-30-cm) flameproof dish with the remaining 1 tablespoon butter.

Bring the water for cooking the pasta to a boil and add the peas. When the water returns to the boil, add your choice of pasta. Cook until al dente, drain and transfer to the prepared dish. Pour the sauce over the top and sprinkle with the cheese.

Slip the baking dish into the broiler and broil (grill) until the top is golden, about 3 minutes. Serve immediately.

Serves 4

Glossary

The following glossary defines terms specifically as they relate to pasta sauces and their preparation. Included are major and unusual ingredients and basic techniques.

ANCHOVIES
Tiny saltwater fish, related to sardines, most commonly found as canned fillets that have been salted and preserved in oil. Imported anchovy fillets packed in olive oil are readily available. Anchovies packed in salt, available canned in some Italian delicatessens, are considered the finest.

ARUGULA
Green leaf vegetable, Mediterranean in origin, with slender, multiple-lobed leaves that have a peppery, slightly bitter flavor. Also known as rocket.

BELL PEPPER
Fresh, sweet-fleshed, bell-shaped member of the pepper family. Also known as capsicum. Most common in the unripe green form, although ripened red or yellow varieties are also available. Creamy pale-yellow, orange and purple-black types can also be found.

BREAD, COARSE COUNTRY
For serving with authentic Italian pasta dishes and for making bread crumbs, choose a good-quality, rustic-style loaf made of unbleached wheat flour, with a firm, coarse-textured crumb. Sold in bakeries, such loaves may also be referred to as country style, rustic or peasant bread.

ARTICHOKES
Also known as globe artichokes. The large flower buds of a type of thistle, grown primarily in the Mediterranean and in California. The tightly packed cluster of tough, pointed, prickly leaves conceal tender, gray-green flesh at the vegetable's center—the heart.

An artichoke is easily prepared for cooking. While trimming, dip artichoke repeatedly in a mixture of water and lemon juice to prevent discoloring.

1. Cut or snap off the artichoke's stem at the base.

2. Cut off approximately 1 inch (2.5 cm) from the top of the artichoke.

3. Starting at the base, break off the toughest outer leaves, snapping them downward.

For an artichoke heart, continue snapping off leaves until only a cone of them remains. Cut these off to reveal the prickly choke; scrape it out. Pare off the remaining tough green outer skin.

CABBAGE, SAVOY
Firm, round, fine-flavored variety of cabbage with dark green leaves marked by a fine lacy pattern of veins.

CANNELLINI BEANS
Italian variety of small, white, thin-skinned, oval beans. Great Northern or small white (navy) beans may be substituted.

CAPERS
Small, pickled buds of a bush common to the Mediterranean, used whole as a savory flavoring or garnish.

CAVIARS & ROES
All manner of fish eggs, or roes, are preserved with salt, which highlights their subtle, briny flavor. The term *caviar* is traditionally reserved for sturgeon roe, which is the finest of the fish roes. Other commonly available roes are carp roe and salmon roe. A good selection may be found in some specialty-food stores and delicatessens.

CAYENNE PEPPER
Very hot ground spice derived from dried cayenne chili peppers.

CHICK-PEAS
Round, tan-colored member of the pea family, with a slightly crunchy texture and nutlike flavor. Also known as garbanzo beans or ceci beans.

CHILI PEPPER
Chilies may be added judiciously to pasta sauces to provide subtle or stronger spiciness. Pure seasoning of ground dried chili peppers, ranging in strength from mild to hot, is available in jars in food market spice sections, as well as in small cellophane packets in ethnic food sections or Latino or Asian markets. Whole ripened and dried red chilies, sold in the same places, can also be used.

CREAM
The terms *light* and *heavy* describe cream's butterfat content and related richness. Light cream, not available everywhere under this name, has a butterfat level varying from 18–30 percent. It is sometimes called coffee cream or table cream. If unavailable substitute equal parts heavy cream and half-and-half. Heavy cream has a butterfat content of at least 36 percent. For the best flavor and cooking properties, purchase fresh cream, avoiding long-lasting varieties that have been processed by ultraheat methods. In Britain, light cream is also known as single cream; use double cream for heavy cream.

EGGPLANT
Vegetable-fruit, also known as aubergine, with tender, mildly earthy, sweet flesh. The shiny skins of eggplants vary in color from purple to red and from yellow to white, and their shapes range from small and oval to long and slender to large and pear shaped. The most common variety, sometimes known as the globe eggplant, is large, purple and globular; but slender, purple Asian eggplants (below), more tender and with fewer, smaller seeds, are available with increasing frequency in food stores and vegetable markets.

CHEESES

In its many forms, cheese makes an excellent ingredient in or garnish for pasta. For the best selection and finest quality, buy cheese from a well-stocked food store or delicatessen that offers a wide variety and has a frequent turnover of product.

Emmenthaler

Variety of Swiss cheese with a firm, smooth texture, large holes, and a mellow, slightly sweet and nutty flavor.

Goat Cheese

Most cheeses made from goat's milk are fresh and creamy, with a distinctive sharp tang; they are sold shaped into small rounds or logs (below). Some are coated with pepper, ash or mixtures of herbs, which mildly flavors them. Also known by the French term *chèvre*.

Gorgonzola

Italian variety of creamy, blue-veined cheese.

Gruyère

Variety of Swiss cheese with a firm, smooth texture, small holes and a relatively strong flavor.

Jarlsberg

Norwegian variety of cheese resembling Swiss Emmenthaler, but with a slightly sweeter flavor.

Mozzarella

Rindless white, mild-tasting Italian variety of cheese traditionally made from water buffalo's milk and sold fresh. Commercially produced and packaged cow's milk mozzarella is now much more common, although it has less flavor. Look for fresh mozzarella sold immersed in water.

Parmesan

Thick-crusted Italian cow's milk cheese with a sharp, salty, full flavor resulting from at least two years of aging. Buy in block form, to grate fresh as needed, rather than already grated. The finest Italian variety is designated parmigiano-reggiano.

Pecorino

Italian sheep's milk cheese, sold either fresh or aged. Two of its most popular aged forms are pecorino romano and pecorino sardo; the latter cheese is tangier than the former.

Provolone

Italian whole-milk cheese, fairly firm in texture and pale yellow in color, with a slightly sweet and smoky flavor.

Ricotta

Very light, bland Italian cheese made from twice-cooked milk—traditionally sheep's milk, although cow's milk ricotta is far more common. Made from the whey left over from making other cheeses, commonly mozzarella and provolone.

FENNEL

Crisp, refreshing, mildly anise-flavored bulb vegetable (below), sometimes called by its Italian name, *finocchio.* Another related variety of the bulb is valued for its fine, feathery leaves and stems, which are used as a fresh or dried herb, and for its small, crescent-shaped seeds, dried and used as a spice.

LEEKS

Sweet, moderately flavored member of the onion family, long and cylindrical in shape with a pale white root end and dark green leaves. Select firm, unblemished leeks, small to medium in size. Grown in sandy soil, the leafy-topped, multilayered vegetables require thorough cleaning.

MARSALA

Amber Italian wine, available both dry and sweet, from the area of Marsala, in Sicily.

MUSHROOMS

With their meaty textures and rich, earthy flavors, mushrooms are used to enrich many pasta sauces. Cultivated white and brown mushrooms are widely available in food markets and greengrocers; in their smallest form, with their caps still closed, they are often descriptively called button mushrooms. Shiitakes, meaty-flavored Asian mushrooms, have flat, dark brown caps usually 2–3 inches (5–7.5 cm) in diameter and are available fresh with increasing frequency, particularly in Asian food shops; they are also sold dried, requiring soaking in warm water to cover for approximately 20 minutes before use. Porcini, a widely used Italian term for *Boletus edulis* and also known by the French term *cèpes,* are popular wild mushrooms with a rich, meaty flavor. Most commonly sold in dried form in Italian delicatessens and specialty-food shops, they are reconstituted in liquid as a flavoring for sauces, soups, stews and stuffings. Portobello mushrooms have wide, flat, deep-brown caps with a rich, mildly meaty taste and a silken texture; growing in popularity, they are available in well-stocked stores.

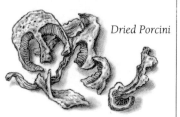

Dried Porcini

OLIVE OIL, EXTRA-VIRGIN

Extra-virgin olive oil, extracted from olives on the first pressing without use of heat or chemicals, is valued for its distinctive fruity flavor. Many brands, varying in color and strength of flavor, are now available; choose one that suits your taste. The higher-priced extra-virgin olive oils usually are of better quality. Store in an airtight container away from heat and light.

OLIVES

Throughout Mediterranean Europe, ripe black olives are cured in combinations of salt, seasonings, brines, vinegars and oils to produce pungently flavored results. Good-quality cured olives, such as French Niçoise or Greek Kalamata or Italian Gaeta varieties, are available in ethnic delicatessens, specialty-food shops and well-stocked food stores. Green olives, picked in their unripened state and cured in brine, are sometimes preferred for their sharper flavor; pitted, they are occasionally stuffed with strips of pickled red pimientos for a hint of color and sweetness.

PANCETTA
Italian-style bacon cured with salt and pepper. May be sold flat or rolled into a large sausage shape. Available in Italian delicatessens and specialty-food stores.

PARSLEY, FLAT-LEAF
Variety of the popular fresh herb with broad, flat leaves that have a more pronounced flavor than the common curly-leaf type. Also known as Italian parsley.

PEPPERCORNS
Pepper, the most common of all savory spices, is best purchased as whole peppercorns, to be ground in a pepper mill as needed, or coarsely crushed. Pungent black peppercorns derive from slightly underripe pepper berries, whose hulls oxidize as they dry. Milder white peppercorns come from fully ripened berries, with the husks removed before drying. Sharp-tasting unripened green peppercorns are sold in water, pickled in brine or dried.

PROSCIUTTO
Italian-style raw ham, a specialty of Parma, cured by dry-salting for one month, followed by air-drying in cool curing sheds for half a year or longer.

RADICCHIO
Leaf vegetable related to Belgian endive (chicory/witloof). The most common variety has a spherical head, reddish purple leaves with creamy white ribs, and a mildly bitter flavor. Other varieties are slightly tapered and vary a bit in color. Also called red chicory.

PASTAS
More than 400 distinct commercial pasta shapes exist. Some of the more common ones, used in this book, include:

Angel Hair
Thin strands—*capelli d'angelo* in Italian.

Armoniche
Ridged pastas shaped to resemble small harmonicas.

Bucatini
Hollow, spaghettilike rods, also known as perciatelli.

Farfalle
"Butterflies." Also called bow ties (below).

Fedelini
Thin spaghetti.

Fettuccine
"Ribbons," popular in both egg and spinach varieties.

Fusilli
Short, twisted strands (below left), also known as eliche or spirali, as well as long, twisted strands (below right).

Garganelli
Small, ridged folded tubes.

Gemelli
"Twins." Short intertwined strands (below).

Gnocchi
Term for small dumplings, usually made of potato dough, and for small dumpling-shaped pasta.

Linguine
"Small tongues." Long, thin, flat strands.

Macaroni
Small to medium short, curved tubes.

Orecchiette
Ear-shaped pasta (below).

Pappardelle
Flat ribbons of fresh pasta, usually about 1¼ inches (3 cm) wide.

Penne
"Quills." Tubes of regular or spinach pasta with angled ends resembling pen nibs. Available smooth and ridged (*rigate*).

Radiatori
"Radiators." Small, ridged shapes (below).

Rigatoni
Moderately sized ridged tubes.

Ruote
Wheels. Also known as rotelle.

Shells
Called *conchiglie* (conch shells) in Italian. Available in various sizes.

Spaghetti
Classic round strands.

Tagliatelle
Fresh pasta rolled very thin and cut into ribbons about ⅜ inch (1 cm) wide (below).

Taglierini
Small, narrow ribbons about ⅛ inch (3 mm) wide.

ROMANO BEANS
Flat, flavorful Italian variety of green beans, similar to runner beans. Sometimes called Italian beans.

SAFFRON
Intensely aromatic, golden orange spice made from the dried stigmas of a species of crocus; used to perfume and color many classic Mediterranean and East Indian dishes. Sold either as threads—the dried stigmas—or in powdered form. Look for products labeled pure saffron.

SALMON, SMOKED
Purchase smoked salmon freshly sliced from a good-quality delicatessen. Lox, which is a salt-cured salmon, and Nova, which is a cold-smoked salmon, are commonly sold in Jewish delicatessens; they have oilier textures and in most cases are not acceptable substitutions for smoked salmon.

SALT, COARSE
Coarse-grained salt, sold in the seasonings section of food stores, is frequently used in marinades and seasonings. Sea salt is an acceptable substitute.

SAUSAGE, ITALIAN SWEET
Fresh Italian sausage is generally made from ground (minced) pork, seasoned with salt, pepper and spices. Those made in the style of northern Italy are usually sweet and mild, sometimes flavored with **fennel** seeds. Southern-style sausages, such as Neapolitan varieties, tend to be

TOMATOES
During summer, when tomatoes are in season, use the best red or yellow sun-ripened tomatoes you can find. At other times of year, plum tomatoes, sometimes called Roma or egg tomatoes, are likely to have the best flavor and texture; for cooking, canned whole plum tomatoes are also good. Small cherry tomatoes, barely bigger than the fruit after which they are descriptively named, also have a pronounced flavor that makes them ideal candidates for quick pasta sauces during their peak summer season.

1. To peel fresh tomatoes, first bring a saucepan of water to a boil. Using a small, sharp knife, cut out the core from the stem end of the tomato. Then cut a shallow X in the skin at the tomato's base.

2. Submerge for about 20 seconds in the boiling water, then remove and dip in a bowl of cold water.

3. Starting at the X, peel the skin from the tomato, using your fingertips and, if necessary, the knife blade.

4. To seed a tomato, cut it in half crosswise. Squeeze gently to force out the seed sacks.

Sun-Dried Tomatoes
When sliced crosswise or halved, then dried in the sun, tomatoes develop an intense, sweet-tart flavor and a pleasantly chewy texture that enhance savory recipes. Available either packed in oil or dry, in specialty-food shops and well-stocked food stores.

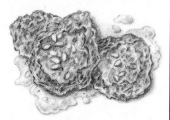

hotter, often flavored with flakes of dried **chili pepper.**

SCALLOPS, SEA
Large variety of the bivalve mollusk with rounds of flesh about 1½ inches (4 cm) in diameter.

SWISS CHARD
Also known as chard or silverbeet, a leafy dark green vegetable with thick, crisp white or red stems and ribs. The green part, often trimmed from the stems and ribs, may be cooked like spinach, and has a somewhat milder flavor.

TROUT, SMOKED
Sold in specialty-food stores and delicatessens, either in fillets or as whole fish requiring skinning and boning, smoked trout has a mild, sweet flavor and moist, tender texture. The skin peels away easily from the smoked fish, and the spine pulls out easily by hand once the two halves of the fish have been separated; use your fingers or tweezers to pick out any remaining small bones.

TUNA, CANNED
Most domestic brands of tuna are packed in water or vegetable oil. Imported tunas, mostly from Italy, are packed in olive oil, which gives the fish a more complex yet delicate flavor that suits it to use in Italian-style recipes such as pasta toppings.

ZEST
Thin, brightly colored, outermost layer of a citrus fruit's peel, containing most of its aromatic essential oils—a lively source of flavor.

Index

ACKNOWLEDGMENTS

The publishers would like to thank the following people and organizations for their generous assistance and support in producing this book:
Sharon C. Lott, Stephen W. Griswold, Ken DellaPenta, Jennifer Mullins, Jennifer Hauser, Tarji Mickelson, the buyers for Gardener's Eden,
and the buyers and store managers for Hold Everything, Pottery Barn and Williams-Sonoma stores.

The following kindly lent props for the photography:
Biordi Art Imports, Candelier, Fillamento, Fredericksen Hardware, J. Goldsmith Antiques,
Sue Fisher King, Lorraine Puckett, RH, and Chuck Williams.